how to have a
happy toddler

how to have a happy toddler

Responding to your child's emotional needs from 0–4

Dr Carol Valinejad

hamlyn

An Hachette Livre UK Company

First published in Great Britain in 2007 by Hamlyn,
a division of Octopus Publishing Group Ltd,
2–4 Heron Quays, London E14 4JP

Copyright © Octopus Publishing Group Ltd 2007

Distributed in the United States and Canada by
Sterling Publishing Co., Inc.
387 Park Avenue South, New York, NY 10016–8810

ISBN-13: 978-0-600-61601-6
ISBN-10: 0-600-61601-0

A CIP catalogue record of this book is available from the
British Library.

Printed and bound in Italy
10 9 8 7 6 5 4 3 2 1

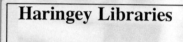

Contents

Introduction

Children are happy when they are given every opportunity and encouragement to flourish as they should, learning and exploring in a nurturing environment in which they know they are loved unconditionally.

The preschool years are a time of rapid development, when children need to achieve a level of progress that will serve them for the rest of their lives. Children have the potential to achieve most of what they need to know emotionally, socially and intellectually by the age of 5 years, but need the right environment that will unleash this potential. An environment that allows them to express their emerging independence, and one that meets their physical, emotional, social and spiritual needs, is the perfect recipe for this.

Unfortunately, an alarming number of children are not achieving their potential, and various reasons have been suggested to explain this, from economics to parenting styles to the conflicting demands of today's society. Mothers and fathers who adopt a distant role, either intentionally or through lack of confidence as parents, can create an emotional distance with their children. Parents who work inordinately long hours, whether of necessity or desire, may inhibit their children's social and emotional development, but the underlying cause is not poverty or affluence but failing to give them the right amount and sort of attention.

Many circumstances have the potential to create stress in children, so the right balance needs to be achieved within families for there to be a good match between allowing children to reach their potential and the needs of parents. Paying attention to raising happy children is especially important in the current climate, as children seem to be exposed to more stress now than they used to.

In recent times, a lot of research has been focusing on the role of happiness in the lives of individuals. In general, happiness has been found to help children maintain a good level of physical and mental health, to enhance emotional resilience, to trigger an upward spiral of being successful and to help children be more creative. In sum, a happy child will become a healthy and successful adult.

Covering the nature of unconditional love, positive attention and respecting others, this book addresses common concerns and is packed with practical advice on communicating with your toddler, managing emotions and guiding your toddler towards independence. It explains ways in which parents can raise happy, confident and well-adjusted children in the formative years of their lives, and at the same time offers some suggestions for how parents can meet their own needs, because it is impossible for parents to meet their children's needs unless they can meet their own first. Here are the vital ingredients that will help your baby develop into a happy toddler and lay the foundations for the very best social and emotional advantage in later life.

Children are happiest when they are allowed to express themselves in ways that come naturally to them.

Understanding the happiness formula

What is happiness?

Happiness is easy to recognize but not so easy to define. It involves contentment but also satisfaction at achievement, an uplifting emotional response to a successful state of life. But what does this mean for a baby or toddler in practical terms?

Ask anyone what they wish for their child, and health and happiness will come out tops, but what do parents actually mean when they say that they know when their child is happy? Some common examples given as indicators of happiness include: 'He is happy to play on his own', 'She is keen to be helpful', 'He laughs a lot and seeks cuddles', 'She enjoys going to nursery', 'He doesn't wet himself', 'She will go to sleep happily', 'He is contented to sit in his pram', 'She feeds and eats well', 'He enjoys

Children are naturally curious about the world around them, so they will ask questions to aid their understanding.

the company of other children', 'She will talk a lot and ask lots of questions'.

Children find value in being allowed to achieve their potential at every stage of their lives. During early childhood a child needs to develop a sense of trust and security with his caregivers and a sense of autonomy. The examples identified by parents above are a reflection of achieving this.

Children are active participants of their environment, and naturally crave knowledge. They seek to explore and to ask lots of questions to make sense of the world. They are not passive recipients, so to be happy, children need to be allowed to take the lead in their learning.

Sadly, millions of children worldwide suffer distorted intellectual, social and emotional delay in their early years because their developmental needs are being neglected. When poverty puts stress on families to the point where all energies are put into basic survival, there is often too little time left over to pay adequate attention to developmental needs. Ironically, wealth and the pursuit of ever more wealth can equally lead to developmentally deprived children: the 'poor little rich girl'. But even the majority of parents, neither dirt-poor nor living in the lap of luxury, find that time is a very precious commodity of which they have too little.

Some benefits of being happy

The sense of wellbeing that happiness provides has positive benefits emotionally and also physically.

So what are the medicinal properties of happiness? Happiness can enhance the body's defences against the potential causes of illness. In contrast, anxious and stressed people are prone to colds and 'flu. Some individuals who have to cope with depression have been found to develop cancer or heart disease.

Interestingly, happiness enhances creativity and divergent thinking. It appears that happiness can stimulate new ideas. New research has also shown that happy individuals persist longer at a task that is not very enjoyable in itself, are better at multi-tasking and are more systematic and attentive.

In addition, research shows that happy people are more likely to be successful in their relationships and

A sign that children are happy is when they know how to use their time constructively.

work performance, to have good mental health and to live longer. Creating happiness in children from early on is not only essential for their learning but is also a crucial investment for their future success.

Why are some children happier than others?

Happy children come from happy homes. Children learn to be happy by what they observe and feel around them, and when they receive the support and approval that gives them the confidence to try new skills.

To some extent, happiness is said to be genetically determined; we all have a basic reserve that remains relatively stable throughout our life, even if events boost it or drain it from time to time. But, while children can inherit a happy outlook on life from their parents, a more significant proportion of happiness can be determined by circumstances and voluntary control. For the very young, a happy child comes from a happy home, whatever the family set-up.

A happy environment

Stress can threaten the happiness of any home. When parents get stressed, then children will be affected. The potential sources of stress that affect children include parental disharmony, being unwanted at birth and inappropriate parenting styles.

Happy children come from homes that meet their emotional, social, spiritual and intellectual needs adequately.

Research shows that children can be affected emotionally from the time they are in the womb. In addition, stressed children, like stressed adults, produce the stress hormone cortisol, which can affect memory, and as a consequence children can develop behavioural difficulties.

Conversely, research has found that when children come from homes where stress is managed well, so that the child is cushioned from it, they have more advanced social skills, do better in school, aren't as likely to succumb to depression during stressful times and play up less than children in homes where stress is not well managed.

When children grow up in a home that feels safe instead of tense, they are better able to cope with life's smaller disappointments. They also tend to approach the world in a much more positive way.

Learning about life

During the first five years, children have an enormous amount to achieve: development on every front takes place at a faster rate than at any other time in their lives. In these few crucial years they need to grow, not only physically and intellectually but also emotionally and socially, learning about their feelings and about appropriate behaviour.

How successfully this is done will affect them for the rest of their lives. Children are happy when their home environment is set up to help them unleash all their potential.

Receiving support and approval

Children need their parents' approval to help motivate them and to know when they are doing things right. They learn to associate certain types of behaviour with parental approval, and these will become strengthened and established over time.

A home where children's reasonable requests are granted and approved will allow them to find out what they are good at, and to develop skills that will

Children can learn a lot about life and develop their creativity when they are allowed to be curious.

help them once they start school. For example, you can encourage your children's inherent creativity whenever they ask for help in carrying out a task, such as putting on a performance. They may request that you form part of the audience or help them find costumes. Mastering the skill of performing in front of an audience begins by practising in the safe, positive atmosphere of home.

Children are happy when their parents help them to achieve their goals, and it gives them the message that what they are doing is valued and important. In contrast, children who have requests turned down frequently, perhaps because their parents may be too busy to take notice, will soon grow discouraged, and may give up asking. This could lead to them being at a disadvantage in their learning in comparison with peers who come from homes where their goals are supported.

Physical development

Although all children go through more or less the same stages, they do it in different ways. Children also develop at their own pace. What is important is not how your child compares with others or with a standard for her age, but that she is moving forward at her own pace and that she is well and happy.

Physical development	Motor and co-ordination skills
0–3 months	
• Will sleep a lot. • Will need feeding frequently. • Will start to develop head control.	• Will start to smile at people. • Will start to look at moving objects and turn head towards noises. • Will start to explore objects with mouth.
3–6 months	
• Will develop better head control and may hold up head when lying on front. • Will start to distinguish between night and day.	• Will reach out for and grasp objects and transfer them from one hand to the other. • May start to roll from side to side and on to front. • May be able sit up if supported. • May start to move around the floor.
6–12 months	
• Will begin teething. • Will start to experience a wide range of food and develop the ability to chew finger foods. • Will change sleep patterns and may sleep for longer at night.	• Will be more mobile and able to control actions better. • Will be able to sit unaided and to crawl effectively. • May be able to walk along by holding furniture, so you will need to move objects out of reach. • Will spend time exploring objects with hands and is able to pick up small objects. • Will start to use objects correctly.

Physical development	Motor and co-ordination skills

12–18 months

- Will continue to teethe.
- Will reduce daytime naps and may sleep through the night.
- May interact with adults by waving goodbye and clapping hands.

- Should be able to walk without help and will start to negotiate stairs.
- Will learn to feed using a spoon.
- May start to scribble but will have limited control over crayons.
- Will start to manipulate toys and objects by picking them up and carrying them or by pushing or pulling objects.
- Able to stack two blocks and roll a ball on request.

About 2 years

- Will have almost full set of teeth.
- May start toilet training.

- Will be competent at getting around and can manage climbing and descending stairs.
- Has greater control over movements – will feed with a spoon and use crayons with more control.
- Will be able to turn the pages of a book and stack several objects in constructive play.

About 3 years

- Will look taller and more like a child.
- Will have full set of teeth.
- May be independent in toilet habits.

- Will be able to walk with complete confidence.
- Can jump over small objects and climb well.
- Can catch, bounce and throw a ball easily.
- Will be able to stack 10 or more blocks and thread small beads.
- Can hold a pencil properly and draw basic shapes.

About 4 years

- Will be independent in most self care-skills – can dress, brush teeth, comb hair and wash with little or no assistance from caregivers.

- Will be able to feed with knife, fork and spoon.
- Will be able to build and create things.
- Will be able to participate in organized games.

Social and emotional development

Children's social and emotional development occurs within the context of their circumstances. The rate at which this unfolds depends very much on the types of experiences to which they are exposed. For example, a child who is used to mixing with a lot of people from early on might show signs of social interaction earlier than a child who isn't.

Social and emotional development	Language and communication

0–3 months

- Will like to be cuddled and enjoys attention.
- Will cry if left alone or unhappy.
- Will develop a broad range of facial expressions.
- Will start to explore the environment and put objects in mouth.

- Will communicate by cooing and babbling.
- Will react to sudden noises.
- Will recognize parents' voices.

3–6 months

- Will start to laugh when happy.
- Will chuckle at simple games.
- Will enjoy attention and the company of people but may start to be shy with strangers.

- Will begin to react to different sounds.
- Will cry to get attention.
- Will make lots of babbling and gurgling noises when playing.

6–12 months

- May show signs of attachment to one parent by crying if you leave him and by showing fear of strangers or unfamiliar situations.
- Will show evidence of being sensitive to other children's moods.
- Will show a preference for different foods and favourite toys.
- Wants to be praised for accomplishment.

- Will begin to understand simple requests.
- Will imitate sounds and will babble in a purposeful way.
- May start to say a few words.
- Will laugh more frequently.
- Will be able to imitate gestures and facial expressions.

Social and emotional development

Language and communication

12–18 months

- Will show growing independence but may still get upset when separated from you.
- Likes to interact with people by being held, listening to stories and giving them objects.
- Can recognize himself in pictures and mirrors.
- Will be able to play alone with toys but will also start to interact with other children.

- Will increase communication skills and start to use a range of words.
- May start to put words together.
- Will be able to understand and follow instructions more easily.
- Will enjoy applause and having an audience.

About 2 years

- Will like to imitate people and help with simple household tasks.
- Will like to watch, observe and learn.
- Will tend to be very sociable and is less shy with strangers.
- May be limited in ability to share.

- Will be able to communicate more clearly and can follow simple instructions.
- Will enjoy making others laugh.

About 3 years

- Will like playing with other children and able to share most of the time and take turns.
- Will like to seek adult approval.
- Will like to pretend play.
- May start to show fear of a situation such as the dark and will start to understand danger.

- Can communicate using sentences.
- Will understand almost everything heard.
- Will become curious about environment and persistently asks 'why?'.
- Will express anger verbally rather than physically.
- Can obey simple rules.

About 4 years

- Will be more independent and may refuse help.
- Will be able to cope with separation from parent.
- Will show caring for other children in distress.
- Will be interested in more complicated pretend play.
- Will become socially aware – wants to be liked and feels hurt if called names.
- May have one or two best friends.
- Will be able to accept fair punishment.
- May become competitive with boys and girls tending to play less with each other.

- Will enjoy having a conversation with adults rather than cuddles.
- Will be eager to please and asks for instructions.
- Will talk freely to other children.
- Will be able to describe events and people.

POSITIVE PARENTING

Nurturing emotional intelligence

Emotions impact on just about everything in life, from relationships to productivity, creativity and achievement. Our ability to handle our feelings also affects our ability to cope with any problems that come our way.

What is emotional intelligence?

Emotional intelligence (sometimes known as emotional literacy) is the ability to recognize and control one's own emotions, as well as to read and respond to those of others. Every baby is born with the capacity for emotional intelligence but how this particular capacity develops depends on the kinds of relationships children have, initially with the adults who care for them. Emotional intelligence is the emotional equivalent of IQ (and is also referred to as EQ), and psychologists generally identify five types of emotional intelligence:

♥ **Awareness of emotions** This is the ability to recognize our own feelings, for example happy, sad, frustrated, angry or bored.

How parents can help Talking to children with an open dialogue and reflective listening will help them explore and open up about their feelings.

♥ **Managing emotions** This involves being able to keep emotions in check, to behave in appropriate ways, to cheer oneself up after a big setback or to control anger.

How parents can help Babies and toddlers need to be taught ways of reassuring and soothing themselves when they are anxious or angry, and positive parenting goes hand in hand with establishing a secure emotional base. Young children also need to learn that feeling has its value and significance – the ratio of comfortable to painful feelings determines how happy we feel with our life.

Children who experience positive parenting learn to respect other people's feelings and find it easier to get along.

♡ **Self-motivation** Harnessing our emotions helps us be happy by allowing us to focus, identify our aims and reach our personal goals.
How parents can help Teaching your boisterous preschooler to direct his energy positively and delay gratification allows him to develop self-discipline.

♡ **Empathy** This involves reading other people's feelings, through body language, tone of voice or facial expression. Even young babies can do this to some extent. We don't have to agree with what the other person thinks, we just need to be accepting of the way they feel.
How parents can help An empathetic response to a child's inner world, to his excitement, frustration and fears, fosters a trusting relationship and helps him to respond sensitively.

♡ **Handling relationships** Emotionally skilled people are usually popular because we enjoy their rapport. They form relationships with other people easily and know how to deal with difficult situations.

When a child's feelings are responded to in an empathetic manner, they will learn to reciprocate this.

How parents can help By teaching social skills, encouraging kindness and co-operation and building confidence and self-esteem.

Research shows

People with high emotional intelligence tend to be socially poised, outgoing and cheerful, are less prone to worrying, are able to express their feelings appropriately and are caring in relationships. They are mostly comfortable in themselves and with others, and happy in their social environment. Emotional health impacts on your child's:

- Mental health
- Physical wellbeing
- Confidence and self-esteem
- Relationships with other people
- Sense of responsibility

EQ – more important than IQ?

Educational psychologists now consider emotional intelligence to be as important – if not more so – than cognitive ability for success at school and in the wider world. Research shows that the emotional abilities little children acquire in the first few years of life make up the essential foundations for learning. Almost all students who perform poorly in school lack one or more of the elements of emotional intelligence.

Children who are confident and optimistic and receive plenty of encouragement and praise for their achievements are far more likely to be successful not only in school but also in later life. Creating a secure base from babyhood and nurturing a high level of emotional intelligence in your children through positive parenting is the best way to ensure that they become happy, responsible adults.

Parents' needs

Successful parenting occurs when parents can address their own needs as well as their children's. Parents suffering from feelings of self-doubt, neglect, exhaustion or inadequacy – or all of these – will affect their child.

As a parent of a young child you will be presented with a range of challenges, especially in the child's first year. Your sleep pattern will be severely disturbed, and you will have to tolerate a less orderly and tidy house. You may have had to give up your job, and as a consequence be living a lifestyle that is less than you are used to. You may not be able to go out on your own or with your partner as often as before; you may have to change your plans last minute; and it could be that you have to put some of your interests on hold. You may also experience differing degrees of depression after giving birth.

In the main, two pervasive feelings – tiredness and depression – can lead to all these challenges becoming overwhelming, so let's explore how they can be dealt with.

Managing tiredness

The simple answer is to rest, but this is not always easy with one or more young children.

The first step is to be able to recognize when you are tired, so that you know when to act. When a group of parents was asked how they knew when they were tired, these were some of their comments: 'Everything is such an effort', 'I feel I have too few reserves', 'I cry for no reason', 'I feel low, irritable and snappy', 'I feel giddy/ache', 'I go very quiet and still', 'I become fussy and abrupt towards

When parents meet their own needs first, then they are more able to meet their children's needs.

others', 'I nod off', 'I become frantically busy and aggressive', 'it feels as everything is getting on top of me', 'I forget things'.

The second step is to understand what is causing your tiredness. Is it purely lack of sleep from broken nights? Or is it worry or tension? Or might it be lack of energy from not eating well, or from trying to do too much?

The third step is to deal with it. First, deal with those factors that are straightforward to change, then tackle the more challenging factors. For example:
• Make sure you are eating as well as you can, especially if you are breastfeeding.
• Cut down on caffeinated and alcoholic drinks late at night.

Second, be realistic and work around what you can't change:
• Accept that you may not be able to do as much in a day as you used to.
• Make allowances for how physically exhausting non-physical things like worry and breastfeeding are.
• Accept that your sleep schedule will be different for a while – take every opportunity during the day to make up for what you have lost at night.

Nipping depression in the bud

Depression is a label used to describe a state of having a very low mood. You may have heard that depression can be an inevitable consequence of childbirth, because it could be a direct result of a chemical imbalance in the brain. This assertion can leave some woman feeling powerless because they think that there is nothing they can do about how they feel, and instead become a passive victim. They may decide to take antidepressants, which for some become addictive.

Depression feeds off itself, therefore recognizing it early so it can be nipped in the bud can help you avoid the 'baby blues' spiralling downward into the black hole of depression or negative thinking.

Getting your child involved in helping you around the house can be a positive and fun way for you to bond.

As soon as you feel your mood becoming low, try to find its cause. Isolation? Worry you're not being a good parent? Loss of control over your life? Loss of a way of life you enjoyed? Think about how some of the following might apply to you and make life better:

Tiredness lowers your reserves of optimism, so look again at some of those examples above and ensure you are getting as much rest as possible.

Develop a new network of friends who also have children. This will naturally evolve as you attend community activities on offer to parents and children.

Start to think creatively about how you can replace what has been lost or at least minimize the impact of it. There may be opportunities for you to do some meaningful work from home.

Start to combine your children's activities with doing something for yourself. For example, you may have been a very active person who enjoyed exercise, so instead of going to the gym, you can take your baby out for a long stroll in the pram.

Time management

A source of stress for many parents is feeling they 'can't get anything done', and that they can't find time to spend with one another. To avoid this, time needs to be managed effectively so that you can create the right atmosphere for your child's and your happiness.

Getting things done

Having a young child around can radically change your usual routine and the way you manage your time and affairs. A balance needs to be made between spending quality time with your child and doing the domestic chores.

Getting children involved in helping out can provide a perfect opportunity to have quality time together.

Successful time management means being left with the feeling that you have achieved something. You might want to start your day with the question:

'What needs to happen today for me to feel like I've had a good day?' Or 'What needs to happen today that will make me feel that I've achieved something?' To start your day with these questions will help you to drive it in the direction that you hope for. Once you know what the answer to these questions will look like, you can then make a provisional plan and hope for the best. However, as consistently failing to achieve what you set up to do can be demoralizing, follow up your initial answers with a fall-back position, and ask yourself 'If I can't do all of this, what will I settle for?'

By managing your own time effectively, you are also teaching your child about time management by example. When they are old enough to understand, this is an important lesson for them, as it will cause them to learn that time has to be made for everything, and on some occasions it may not directly relate to their wishes.

When time for yourself is limited, doing solitary chores can provide you with a brief moment of often needed respite.

Time for yourself and each other

Solutions to family problems can be found in understanding the nature of how family members interact with one another. The quality of a relationship is enhanced by a couple being in touch with each other, and being aware of one another's needs. In contrast, a couple who loses touch with each other will make their relationship vulnerable to conflict and may have a tendency to misinterpret in a negative way what might be well-intentioned gestures.

So how can a couple go about remaining in touch with one another? It may not be the actual time that you spend together that makes the difference, but what you do with that time that counts.

Accept that you might not be able to spend as much time with each other as you used to, but you can be creative about making one another feel wanted and cherished and involved.

Make sure you continue to show that the other is still special. It is often the small things that have the most influence. Remember what the other likes, and try to do this as much as possible – for example, a favourite meal on a Friday night. Make it a habit to say encouraging things, rather than putting one another down.

Communicate effectively with one another by informing each other of your intentions. For example, communicate what you hope to achieve in a day, and negotiate with one another about how you can help go about this.

Recognize each other's need for solitary activities to be able to replenish your resources and recharge your batteries. Negotiate with each other to be allowed some time for yourself so that you can have something to look forward to.

KEY STRATEGIES

Juggling different needs

Juggling with different needs can present an opportunity for you to discover abilities in yourself that you did not know existed, so begin to welcome the challenge, rather than to see it as a daunting prospect.

There will be times when you feel you cannot possibly accommodate everybody's needs. You may feel that you are either being stretched very thin and doing nothing as wholeheartedly as you would wish, or that different needs are in conflict with each other. Here are 10 strategies that can help you cope.

O━ Address your needs. You cannot meet your children's needs adequately if you neglect your own. For example, if you need a hot drink or to sit still for a little while, don't wait until you have completed a list of chores, as when you have finished, some other need may present itself and you'll run out of resources to cope.

O━ Protect your evenings as sacred time. A useful way to think about having some undisturbed time might be to use your evenings for something you enjoy, once the children have gone to bed.

O━ Adopt a flexible approach. Accept that managing a family and looking after young children is a new phase of life, and you may discover new areas about yourself that you did not know existed. Avoid having a fixed routine, but instead take each moment at a time. Avoid being in a hurry – as long as you know that progress is being made, then you are doing all right.

O━ Team work rather than individual work. Every member of a family can have different tasks that can help contribute to the healthy functioning of the home. This can include: a share in the care of the baby, rather than this being the sole responsibility of one person – it might be the delight of older siblings, for example, to play with their young brother or sister. Generally, other people like to be helpful, so gratefully accept these offers.

Be prompt about seeing to your own needs, otherwise you may run out of inner resources to manage your day.

O⊶ Accept offers of help from others. In addition to receiving help from your immediate family, family and friends may also show willingness to help you out on occasions, for example by babysitting. Again, accept these offers.

O⊶ Allow for different needs. Everyone has needs, but not all needs are the same. While a baby might require a lot of your time, a toddler may be happy doing some things without you, so don't condemn yourself if you think that your time is not divided up equally.

O⊶ Tolerate uncertainty. Uncertainty may arise when you're not sure whether what you have organized will work out. It is always worth trying because an opportunity missed is an opportunity lost.

O⊶ Go with the flow. You may be trying to address your family's needs in a particular way, but may be experiencing some resistance. If so, then abandon the plan for a while or try a slightly different tack. It may well be that a new way of doing things will present itself.

O⊶ Be creative in the kitchen. Cooking for the family is a major task for any household, and you can guarantee that mealtimes will be just the time when every other need possible will present itself. Think creatively by doing some cooking at a quiet time during the day so that you just have to heat it up at mealtimes, or occasionally cook in bulk and freeze, so that meals are ready with minimum fuss when needed.

O⊶ Strategic play. 'Helping' can be an extension of children's playtime. For example, a good game to play is pairing socks and counting them, or unpacking the shopping.

Siblings have a role to play in one another's development, and so will normally enjoy playing together.

Establishing a secure base

Bonding with your baby

The strong attachment between babies and the important people in their life is essential to the success of their emotional and social development. It is this secure attachment that will set them up to cope with adverse events in later life, and, as a consequence, they will become resilient individuals.

As we have seen in *Understanding the happiness formula* (pages 8–25), a happy home is a vital ingredient to creating happiness in your child. Part of this is establishing a successful bonding between parent and infant. When parents are consistently able to understand their baby's signals and respond to her needs, they become more confident in their parenting ability. In fact, it is now widely accepted that children need to bond with at least one adult in the early years in order to trust others, build lasting relationships and feel good about themselves.

Bonding difficulties

For some mothers, this bond does not happen straight away. This can be for a number of reasons, including: an unplanned pregnancy; resentment at having to make a sacrifice you weren't quite ready for (such as giving up your career); feeling over-whelmed by responsibility; relationship difficulties; lack of confidence; having a traumatic birth; and not finding babies interesting. If such feelings feature in your relationship with your child, then it is important to seek help quickly. Parents who experience difficulty bonding with their child will find it difficult to relate to her in a responsive way. Opposite are some suggestions for how parents can facilitate bonding.

Children will respond to caregivers who respond promptly to their signals within the context of unconditional love.

What you can **do**

Spend time enjoying your baby, holding her so that she can experience your warmth and become familiar with your smell. Touch is an important means of communication for babies, and plays a significant role in building parent–child relationships. Baby massage is a good way of enjoying this.

Babies can't be spoilt, so seek to understand the reason behind their crying. For example, is it tiredness, hunger, need for a nappy change?

Babies' sounds have meaning – in addition to crying, there are gurgles and fretting noises. Learning to recognize these and respond to them will show that you understand what they are communicating

Children like to have a routine, so make provision for this. For example, have an outline schedule of when they will go out, have their naps, have a feed and so on. (Bear in mind that routines will change as they grow and if, for example, they are ill.)

Children like to listen to music and be sung to, and these activities can easily fit into a regular routine, such as lying-down time or before bedtime.

Reading to your baby provides an ideal opportunity to be intimate with one another.

What you can **say**

A baby finds her parents' voice soothing, so find things to say to her. Play games, such as 'This little piggy went to market' or 'Incy wincy spider'. Telling stories to your baby is also another good way of enhancing parent–child communication.

Tell your baby that you are aware of their upset. Say: 'Oh, you need your nappy changed' or 'I know it is your dinner time; mummy is just warming it.'

For example, say: 'I know what that means, you're tired now – let me put you to bed.' or 'You're not happy sitting there – let mummy give you a cuddle.'

Use the opportunity to keep her informed about what is taking place as a way of keeping up the communication with her.

Engage her as if you are both singing together. This can be done with or without the aid of age-appropriate music in the background.

Talk about the pictures, and create the sounds – '"Woof, woof," said the dog' – to sustain her interest.

Showing affection

Most babies are cute to look at, inviting you to hold, cuddle and kiss them. Perhaps nature designed it this way, to encourage instinctive parental affection. Your baby will reciprocate when you show affection towards him.

When a baby receives emotional warmth and support, and sensitivity to his needs, he will develop a secure attachment to the person or people providing these signs of affection. Research shows that, generally, babies will direct their love to those who are sensitive to their needs and attend to them quickly, and not just their mothers, as is commonly thought. It is the quality of care given that is important, rather than the status of the caregiver. Fathers, for example, are also attachment figures to whom children can direct their affection.

Father love

In the past fathers used to be viewed as the invisible breadwinner, so in trying to understand child development a lot of attention was given to the mother–child interaction. Now that more men are actively sharing in the task of childcare, researchers have the opportunity to understand the unique contributions that fathers make to the happiness of their children.

One project, based on following 17,000 children at ages 7, 11, 16, 23 and 33, looked at

Young children have a need for intimacy and closeness. They will generally welcome affection and will show it in return – it communicates to them that they are totally accepted.

the influence of fathers on their children's wellbeing. They described an involved father as a father who reads to his child, takes outings with his child, is interested in the child's education and takes an equal role in managing his child. This study found that:

• A good father–child relationship is associated with an absence of emotional and behavioural difficulties in adolescence, and greater academic motivation.

• Teenagers who have grown up feeling close to their fathers go on to have more satisfactory adult relationships with a partner or spouse.

• A good relationship with the father or a father figure can help protect children against adolescent psychological problems in families where the parents have separated.

• Girls whose fathers are involved are less likely to have mental health problems, and are therefore more likely to have happy, fulfilling lives.

? QUESTIONS & ANSWERS

Q I would like to return to work part-time when my baby is 7 months old, but I am worried that this might affect the bonding process between us.

A By 7 months, you and your baby will have already formed a very strong bond, so you needn't worry that this will be affected. What you need to focus on now is allowing your baby to get to know the person who will be looking after him, so that he will be happy to be left for the hours that you will be away. You may have to do this a few months beforehand, leaving him for short periods and gradually increasing the time, until he gets used to being cared for by someone else.

Q My 9-month-old baby cries whenever I try to allow others to hold her. I am worried that she will never be able to get used to being looked after by other people.

A This reaction is quite normal, and what it means is that your baby is securely attached to you. It is possible for your baby to become attached to others if they play an active role in looking after her right from the start, then she will be happy to allow them to hold her. The fact that she is attached to you means that she will develop an increasing ability to form good relationships in the future.

Responding to your child's needs

Responding to your child's needs doesn't mean having to rush to her the moment she cries; it means providing consistent care, protection and emotional support. Parents who combine unconditional love with firmness will respond to their child's needs best.

Children are happy when their needs are met. In addition to having their physical needs of diet, sleep and exercise provided, they need to be protected from harm, accident, abuse and avoidable illness. They also need to feel emotionally secure and have a sense of social well-being. Consistently meeting these needs causes your child to learn to trust you, as you show that you are in tune with her.

Of course, parents will be better able to do this if they are confident about parenting: over-heavy or over-lax styles of parenting are often a sign of lack of confidence. Research identifies four different styles of parenting: authoritative, authoritarian, permissive and neglectful.

Authoritative

Authoritative parenting is characterized by warm, firm expectations of children, and encourages children to think independently, with firm but moderate discipline. This approach is underpinned by the knowledge that children require unconditional love if they are to function at their optimum. It is this parenting style that is advocated in this book, so most of the suggestions outlined throughout reflect this parenting style.

Confident parents will allow their children to experiment in safe ways and to develop their independent thinking.

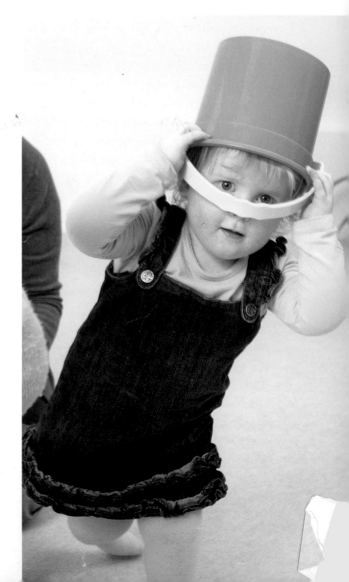

Authoritarian

Authoritarian parenting is characterized by little warmth and respect for the child's individuality, and too much emphasis on firm discipline and making demands. This strict approach to parenting is likely to be underpinned by the view that a disciplinarian stance is necessary to get children to behave in desirable ways.

Inherent beliefs and assumptions are not always easy to change, but parents need to be open to learning about the developing needs of children, and exploring how to relate to their children in ways that have been found to be effective.

Achieving obedience through fear can have a number of limitations: it can prevent a child from experiencing true affection from their parents and hence affect the bonding process; it does not reflect a true understanding of the needs of children, which will cause those needs to be overlooked. As a consequence, the child will become frustrated, but be likely to internalize such feelings because of fear of punishment. This could result in a risk of developing mental health problems, as well as other problems associated with underdeveloped bonding.

Permissive

This style puts too little emphasis on expectations of children, and is overly lenient. Children respond best to positive discipline. Research shows that parental aspirations for their children can affect how successful they will be later on in life. A child whose parents have high expectations of her (while avoiding being too pushy) is likely to achieve more than a child whose parents have few expectations of her.

Children should be credited with more intelligence than is often assumed of them. When they are faced with a challenge, let them feel that you believe they can resolve it, rather than discourage them by putting them off trying. This will help them develop their problem-solving skills.

Setting limits and providing boundaries helps children to feel safe and behave in acceptable ways.

Neglectful

This style of parenting is characterized by minimal warmth and involvement, and has been found to be associated with conduct problems and the development of antisocial behaviour later on, such as street crime.

Neglectful parenting tends to evolve when parents are faced with a lot of social problems, such as mental ill-health, prolonged unemployment or relationship difficulties, as having to cope with these circumstances has an impact on good parenting. Although immediate change is not always possible, these parental needs obviously need to be addressed. Often, admission that there is a problem is the first step of change. Help from close friends and family, and community resources, can be a good way of beginning to address some of the issues that prevent parents from giving their children the love and care they need.

A healthy start

Food is one of the necessities of life. Children can build up strong associations with eating and with specific foods from a very young age, so making those associations happy, healthy ones is an important process.

Feeding baby

Breast milk is the most nutritious first food for a baby (see panel, opposite). Having said that, if you are having difficulty breastfeeding it is important that you don't feel a failure or pressurized into persevering if it's not working for you. Your frustration and tension will communicate itself to your baby.

Whatever the feeding method in the first few months, feeding times provide a good opportunity for you to be close to your baby, to talk to her, cuddle her and build those essential bonds.

The importance of good eating

Parents can have an influence on the foods their children develop a liking for by establishing good eating patterns right from the start, including the choice of foods they feed them when they start eating solids. There are three reasons why this is important for your child:

Children who don't have their nutritional needs met can become irritable or disruptive.

A young child's brain is in a state of rapid development, and it needs adequate nutrition for optimum development.

A child who grows used to having the minimum will always make do with the minimum and so will struggle to develop a good appetite.

When children have positive associations with food they are more likely to enjoy eating a greater variety of healthy foods.

Children will develop a healthy appetite when they are introduced to healthy eating from when they are young.

Healthy eating, healthy development

Judging by the huge range of children-orientated foods around, the overriding message is that our children want to eat lots of sugar, salt and processed foods. And in a way this is true – just like adults, sugar (and savoury processed foods are often high in sugar too) gives them a 'high'. But this energy boost is short-lived, so they soon need more.

But processed foods are stripped of essential nutrients, and insufficient nutrients can result in various kinds of behavioural and learning difficulties. In addition, the sugar and additives can cause mood swings and hyperactivity – an unhealthy diet can seriously damage a child's happiness both in the short and long term. An unhealthy diet can seriously damage a child's happiness. In fact, it has been suggested that inadequate knowledge and inappropriate feeding practices are often a greater determinant of malnutrition than actual lack of food.

? QUESTIONS & ANSWERS

Q I know they say breast is best, but formula milk says it contains all the nutrition a baby needs. How is breast milk better?

A All milks contain water, fat, protein, carbohydrate, minerals and vitamins in varying proportions. Breast milk, however, contains other important factors that are absent from bottled milk; these include hormones, enzymes, growth factors, essential fatty acids and protective factors for the immune system. Breast milk also has many benefits for both mother and child. The benefits to mother include lower risk of ovarian cancer and faster return to pre-pregnancy figure. The benefits to baby include prevention of a range of health problems, such as ear and chest infections and diarrhoea, gastroenteritis and abdominal upsets, and allergic symptoms such as eczema and, later, hay fever.

Q My baby doesn't seem happy with milk alone. When can I start weaning?

A It is now recommended that breastfeeding mothers feed their babies with breast milk exclusively for the first six months, to achieve the optimum benefits described above. Once your baby has reached 6 months, you need to start thinking about weaning her. Starting her on soft purées of fresh fruit and vegetables is a good way of building up her appetite for these foods. Then gradually increase her diet to include fresh meat/fish and carbohydrates, such as rice and potatoes. If you can, continue breastfeeding throughout the weaning period, which can go on until your child is at least 2 years old.

Feeding themselves

When toddlers show signs of wanting to feed themselves, parents should respond positively. Learning to feed yourself is a vital skill and an early expression of independence. You just need to remember that practice makes perfect!

First foods

At around the age of 6 months, start with tiny amounts of puréed food once a day in addition to milk, slowly increasing these tiny tastes to at least three times a day after about two months. Don't introduce too many new flavours all at once, but every few days add to the repertoire. Your child will begin to show you what his favourite flavours are.

Learning the skills

Some toddlers will signal that they are ready to learn by trying to grab the spoon and feed themselves.

Others may not like being fed from a spoon, but want to dive in with their hands. Allow them to participate and help themselves as far as is possible, even if it means that they will make a mess.

If children are not encouraged to express their independence with feeding themselves, they will learn not to try, and you will run the risk of ending up with a 5-year-old who will not have developed sufficient mastery to feed herself.

Coping with the mess

Children need to develop a healthy relationship with and enjoyment of food. If every mealtime becomes a battle over what to eat and how to eat it, a child may carry the association of food and stress into later life. Resign yourself to the fact that feeding a toddler is a messy, time-consuming business. Spread a plastic sheet under the high chair – a plastic overall for yourself might be an inelegant blessing, too – and keep up the encouragement and praise, however messy it gets.

Giving encouragement and praise is important, because children need to be allowed to practise the skill of independent eating in a non-threatening environment. It is only normal that they will not be perfect at it to begin with.

Your toddler will let you know when she is ready to take on the challenge of feeding herself.

What you can **do**

Pay attention to the signs your child gives you that she is ready to feed herself – for example, taking the spoon away from you.

Children vary in how they respond to being weaned. Some may not want to be fed with a spoon. If this is the case, use clean hands instead, and allow her to hold a soft piece of vegetable if she seems ready to do this.

Introduce your baby to new foods regularly but not too many new tastes at once.

Mix her favourite foods with other bland varieties and, as weaning progresses, include finger foods, along with different varieties of foods and different consistencies.

Make eating a social event, and when possible eat at the same time as your child.

Be patient and avoid being in a hurry. Children will gain mastery of their eating in their own time and not before.

What you can **say**

Give her a spoon and praise her for trying. Say: 'Well done. You're feeding yourself with a spoon.' This can be done while you feed her with another spoon.

Avoid conflict by adapting to her way of doing it. Say: 'Good girl' whenever she manages to eat a mouthful of food.

Tell her what she is eating, for example: 'Here, darling, I'm giving you some pear to try.'

Smile encouragingly while she eats, saying: 'hmmm, delicious' to enhance her interest in the food.

Show enthusiasm about eating food. Say: 'This is great, I'm going to have some more.'

Your child will pick up on both non-verbal and verbal communication of encouragement. Say: 'You dropped it. Never mind, you did very well by trying.'

POSITIVE PARENTING

Making the most of mealtimes

Children are generally categorized as 'good eaters' and 'bad eaters'. Those parents with good eaters have nothing to worry about – this is for those parents who are struggling with getting children to eat adequately.

Parents frequently have worries that their toddlers aren't eating enough, or eating the right type of food, or are faddy eaters. Mealtimes should be a relaxed, happy time, but sometimes parental worries can build up to become a greater concern than the child's actual eating habits. Here are some facts about children and their attitude to food that it might be helpful to keep in mind.

♥ **Children's appetites vary** Sometimes children may not be ready to eat at convenient times like the rest of the family.

How parents can help Don't waste time battling over food. Accept that your child is not hungry yet, and if you need to go out, take a healthy snack with you. Be flexible but avoid the promise of something else if he eats his food now.

♥ **Children respond to play** Children can learn to eat adequately and sensibly when play is used as a tool to engage them rather than insisting on obedience.

When children get involved with the preparation of the family meal, they are more likely to become interested in eating.

How parents can help Instead of, for example, announcing lunch as an intrusive break into a game, ask what they are playing and say something to fit into the scenario. For example, if they are playing camping, say: 'Campers, it's time to get out of the tent and have some lunch, because we'll be going for a walk in the woods afterwards.'

♡ **All children like food** Some parents say that their children do not eat, but what they usually mean is that their children are not enthusing over the food they are being offered.

How parents can help Get your child involved in cooking with you – this will motivate him to want to eat his own creation. Obtain a children's cookery book and try out new recipes. Build up a repertoire of favourite foods and, if necessary, mix these with other, blander foods to add variety. All children go through fads that come and go (especially once they start visiting friends' homes or going to playschool), but toddlers aged 3 or under are more receptive to new flavours, so introduce a wide range of suitable tastes while they are still young.

♡ **Children like to count** Once your child can count up to about five, you can begin to incorporate counting games into mealtimes.

How parents can help To make it fun to eat at least five portions of fruit or vegetables a day, say at the beginning of the day: 'Let's count how many times you eat either a fruit or vegetable.' (Five a day, the counting way.) Because he has been given the task of remembering, he'll remind you each time, even when you forget. Younger children can be inspired by aspiration: they need to eat their fruit and vegetables if they want to grow tall and strong.

♡ **Children will eat eventually** If a child refuses to eat, you can either get cross and heavy-handed or take the long view. The disadvantage with

Children will become enthusiastic about eating when they are encouraged to see the fun in it.

the first option is that the child learns to associate eating with conflict, and mealtimes become a dread rather than a pleasure.

How parents can help If, after encouragement, your child is adamant that he does not want the food, then put it aside and say it will be ready for him when he is hungry. Avoid giving sugary snacks instead.

Let's pretend

Playing at being someone or something else can often encourage children who do not eat well. You might play at mice and say: 'Hello, mouse. If you go through your hole, you may find some delicious food waiting for you.' Your child pretends to go through a hole while you hold the food in front of his mouth. Before you know it, all the food on the plate is finished and your child would like more.

Developing good sleep patterns

Sleep is a restorative for mind and body, and children are happy when they get their full quota. Establishing a regular sleep routine makes life sunnier and easier for both parents and child.

Signs of tiredness

During the first few weeks you get to know your baby by observing her and noticing those times when she frets and cries. If other needs, such as nappies and feeding, have been dealt with, then it is likely that she is telling you that she wants to sleep.

Toddlers and preschoolers might show tiredness by becoming irritable, show aggressive behaviour such as hitting at loved ones, and display generally aimless, chaotic behaviour. Research shows that sleep deprivation is linked to aggressive behaviour and sustained sleep deprivation can result in lethargy.

How much sleep?

Children need a lot of sleep – they are going through a lot of neurological change and growth, which is an exhausting process. After a good sleep a baby will look fresh, wake up with a smile on her face and communicate her good mood with a soft cooing.

A newborn baby will need up to 17 hours, as much during the day as at night. In the course of the next few years she will become more amenable to settling into a regular routine, where the daytime sleep becomes less and less until all her sleeping is done at night. A 4-year-old will still need about 12 hours, but almost all at night.

Establishing a routine

Sleepless and broken nights are hard on both parents and children, so a satisfactory sleep routine is very important, although it can take some effort. A regular sequence, such as a quiet hour, a bedtime drink, teeth-cleaning, a story and a set time for bed may need to be adhered to like a ritual, but it will help instil an invaluable routine for a toddler.

Some babies can take months before they settle into a long core sleep at night. But even when very young they can learn the habit of sleeping soundly.

Children will establish good sleep patterns when they learn to associate appropriate comfort symbols with going to bed. For example, reading to wind down.

Q How can I get my 1-year-old daughter to settle down at night and not to cry every time I leave the room?

A Babies discover very quickly if crying always brings cuddles. A technique known as controlled crying follows a regime of checking on your child at increasing intervals (say 5, then 10, then 15 minutes), but just to let her know you are there, not to cuddle or talk. Ignoring the crying is hard and the technique takes persistence, but once she no longer expects night-time crying to be 'rewarded', her nights, and yours, will be much more peaceful.

An alternative technique is useful for toddlers as well as babies. For, say, three nights, stay close until you are sure they are asleep, then over a succession of nights gradually increase your distance – to a chair, to beside the door, but still not leaving the room until they are asleep. It may take a month, but if your retreat has been slow and steady they will be ready to accept your retreat to another room.

Q My son is 3 years old, and he is still reluctant to sleep in his own bed. What can I do to get him to enjoy his own bed?

A Sleep behaviour is often embedded in what children learn to associate with bedtime. Your son has learned to associate going to bed with yourself, and for things to change he will need to learn new associations. Going to bed with you provides him with security and comfort. You need to take a phased approach, rather than an abrupt one, gradually decreasing your time with him, and at the same time compensating with an alternative symbol of comfort and security.

Dealing with nightmares

Nightmares can happen at any age, but are particularly common among toddlers and up to the age of about 6 years. They are thought to be a symptom of daytime struggles associated with growing up.

Nightmares, especially ones in which a child fears being taken away, are very common among young children, and it reflects their preoccupation with separation anxiety. Nightmares are very frightening for young children, especially as they have not yet learned to distinguish between reality and fantasy, and may not yet be able to articulate their experience. The important thing is to give as much reassurance as possible.

In order to reduce the risk of having nightmares, it is important for children to be able to resolve their conflicts when they are awake. You can assist this by helping your toddler to express his concerns throughout the day.

Night terrors

These are a similar but distinct phenomenon. They occur during deep sleep, usually in the early part of the night (nightmares happen during REM or 'dream' sleep, more typically in the second half of the night), and are alarming for you but not for your child. A toddler having a night terror will appear to wake suddenly, apparently terrified and often agitated, screaming or moaning. Unless the agitation is prolonged, the best move is to do nothing – your child will fall back into untroubled sleep and, unlike a nightmare, remember nothing in the morning.

Children should be encouraged to deal with their daytime struggles to decrease the likelihood of having nightmares.

What you can **do**

If you hear screams from your child's room, then go in straight away. If it is a night terror, just wait and wake her gently only if it is prolonged.

Children under the age of 2 years have not yet developed the concept of dreaming, so will need physical comforting. Hold her and comfort her so that she knows she is safe.

Allow your older toddler to describe her dream to you, and listen sympathetically.

Offer the choice of sleeping with the light on or with the door open if this will help. If your child is afraid to go back to sleep, you may need to stay with her for a while.

Do not spend too much time trying to prove to her that the monster is not in her room, by opening cupboards and so on. Just be calm and clear.

If nightmares are frequent, try to find out what might be causing them. Did they start when attending a new playgroup, for example?

What you can **say**

If it is a nightmare, offer cuddles and reassuring words. Don't try to explain or rationalize the nightmare to your child.

Either offer reassuring words, for example 'Everything is all right', or sing her a favourite lullaby or tell her a comforting story.

Show her that you take her seriously by asking her to clarify or describe details of her account that may need expanding.

Explain what you are going to do and say that this will be a comfort and help her sleep easily.

Acknowledge her fear and tell her: 'You're quite safe, and I'll protect you.'

Give reassurance relating to the cause. For example: 'I've noticed that these started when you started playgroup. We'll have to find a way to make these visits easier.'

Helping your child to relax

Being relaxed isn't just about physically doing nothing, it's also about a complete lack of tension, of unadulterated enjoyment, of safely letting go. Allow time for children to luxuriate in having no demands made on them.

Anxiety impedes learning. Children become anxious when they are presented with challenges beyond their capabilities, when they have to respond to unreasonable requests made of them, when they pick up on a tense atmosphere in the home, and if they are subject to abuse in any form. But even children not subject to undue anxiety benefit from time when they can feel in control, are not criticized or told off for minor things, and are allowed to express themselves.

Undemanding playtime

Of course your child has to abide by rules, learn to take others into account and rise to challenges. But he should also know what it is like to feel completely carefree, whether alone or with family and friends. 'Silly' times, full of ecstatic laughter, will fill his memory with nice things and generate a wealth of shared happy memories.

Relaxing with a book

Young children are avid learners and imitators, and even long before they can read will memorize favourite stories and enjoy identifying characters and events in the pictures. At the toddler stage, participating in reading can be an exciting, active pastime, but also a passive relaxation when it involves curling up and being read a familiar story. Allow plenty of both types of reading time.

When children are encouraged to relax, their receptiveness to new learning is greatly enhanced.

Chilling out

Young children need time out from the hustle and bustle of everyday life, just like we do. Opposite are some ideas for 'quiet time'.

What you can **do**

Ensure that you allow time during the week for your child to pursue a quiet activity where he can just chill out.

Listening to music can be very soothing, Help your child develop an appreciation for music by allowing him to listen to music from the time he is a baby.

Massage is an effective way of relaxing. For example, baby massage has been found to be effective in helping babies to develop good sleep routines.

A nice warm bath is relaxing at any age. Bubbles and bath toys encourage lighthearted play.

Provide your child with the space to pursue solitary activities of his choice without being disturbed.

Reading is a relaxing activity, and your child will find reading time with you very enjoyable. It will also foster an interest in reading for himself as he gets older.

What you can **say**

Nothing. Don't let him feel he can't talk to you, but he shouldn't feel pressure to talk either.

Singing together is a great opportunity to relax and enjoy the same thing.

Say soothing, relaxing things to your baby or toddler as you massage. You might talk in rhythm with the massage movements.

This can be a chance to let him tell you about his day or for some silly banter.

Tell him where you will be and that you will be available if he needs you. Advise him of an approximate time when he may need to stop.

Talk about the story to help your child develop his thinking and make associations with the real world.

Just having fun

Having fun provides an opportunity for children to do activities that intrinsically motivate them, which is part of the happiness formula. Children also learn best when they see the fun in what they are doing.

Engaging in activities that your child enjoys contributes to her happiness. Because having fun involves spontaneity and, in the main, is free from external constraints, it means that your child can exercise her strengths, talents and interests in an unlimited way. Older toddlers are very good at finding their own fun, and at the same time are also

appreciative of the efforts made by their parents to organize fun activities for them.

Following their lead
Children enjoy engaging with their parents and feeling they are sharing 'grown-up' activities. It is easy to forget that what are to us everyday, mundane

activities or chores are new and exciting when you are only 3 or 4 years old. Toddlers see lots of potential fun in helping cook or wash the car or rake up leaves. Being responsive to your child's lead about which activities provide her with fun will help you both get the best out of enjoying time together.

Sometimes requests are made at inconvenient times, but go along with their enthusiasm when you can. For example, your child might like to have some fun baking a cake. Your first thought might be to groan inwardly at the mess, but this is outweighed by the advantage of doing an activity together. And after a few baking episodes, you'll find that your toddler will become more adept and can start taking on some tasks by herself, which is good for her confidence and skills, provided it is safe.

Physical fun

Taking children out for recreation is another way of having fun. You will notice that they show excitement by laughing, running around and inviting you to play games with them. Physical exercise, whether it is a ball game, a session at a 'tumbling tots' type gym or just running around outside, is good for them too, although they don't know it (see box).

Helpful hints

As much as possible, support your child in pursuing those activities that she would like to do. Whenever she makes a request she is telling you that this is how she would like to spend her time, and that doing this activity will make her satisfied and will contribute to her happiness.

Notice those occasions when your child is totally absorbed in an activity, and make provision for her to continue. By doing this, you are giving your child time to develop her growing skills.

When children find the fun in learning they will do it again and again.

When children play, they reveal to you what they know about the world.

Take your child to settings where you know that she will enjoy herself, for example to visit friends, on a special trip or to do something such as a sport or a game you know she loves.

Exercise: fun and beneficial

Exercise releases chemicals in the body called endorphins, which give us the 'feel good factor'. As a consequence, when children are exposed to regular exercise they will feel happy. Other benefits linked to exercise include: better general health, increased self-esteem, reduced stress and anxiety, improved mobility, improved muscular strength and endurance, a steady, healthy weight and prolonged life.

Creating the right environment

Children have a great capacity to learn from a very young age, and if their potential for development is to be achieved, they need an environment in which they are encouraged to learn and explore safely.

Children go through a faster rate of development during their first five years than at any other time in their life. By the end of their second year of life, children will have developed thinking skills, most of their attitudes towards learning and a full range of social skills. At the age of 5, the brain has reached 95 per cent of its adult weight and by this time half of the intellectual growth of a child is complete.

A world of words

Research shows that even though a baby can't speak yet, he is learning to talk by listening. A baby's brain is designed to 'mop up' language incredibly quickly, and by the end of his second year, a child has the potential to gain two-thirds to three-quarters of all the language he will ever use in ordinary conversation for the rest of his life. This is why it is important to talk to toddlers a lot every day and for them to hear and see people talking around them.

Everything is part of learning

Children need to be active participants, rather than passive recipients. For toddlers, every aspect of day-to-day life offers an opportunity for them to learn about how the world works and to practise new skills. If you observe them closely, they will let you know what stage they are at in their development. As with the cake-baking example on page 47, it is good to get them involved as far as it is safe to do so.

Safe and secure

Children are naturally inquisitive, so make your home a safe environment in which they can explore and take risks without putting themselves in danger. A lack of opportunity to explore will inhibit your child's later development.

For young children the world should be free not only of physical danger but also of threats to their sense of security. Exposure to social adversity, maltreatment and insecure attachment in early life are all causes of stress, and children function best in an environment where they are cushioned from stress. A supportive, secure environment maximizes their potential for new learning and development.

When children's active participation is encouraged, they have maximum readiness for new learning.

What you can **do**

During the preschool years, children do most of their learning through play, so provide an environment that is rich in play opportunities.

Spend time with your child to relate to her at her level. Be interested in what she says and does and help her to solve problems she encounters.

When possible, avoid communicating concerns and worries to children if they don't need to know about them. They may interpret it as threatening.

Create a physical environment that is safe for your child to explore without too much restriction.

Provide a literate environment, for example labelled pictures pinned up and books to read. Research shows that children who come from homes where their is much exposure to print will be better at developing their literacy skills.

What you can **say**

Say that it is alright to use safe household utensils if it will assist in a game or pretend play.

If you can't respond immediately, let her know when you can, for example, 'When I've finished feeding the baby, I'll come and help you.' Be specific in terms she can understand, rather than talking about elapsed time. For example, '5 minutes' is not meaningful to a toddler.

If your child sees you are upset, acknowledge her observation, but reassure her: 'I'll be all right, don't worry about mummy.'

Although you will remain watchful, minimizing danger to your child will spare you having constantly to say 'Mustn't touch' or 'Don't go there.'

When children see print frequently, they will naturally work out what it reads as they will always make connections. You can, for example, name objects from posters together.

POSITIVE PARENTING

Respecting rules and boundaries

While development comes naturally to children, understanding the rules of behaviour doesn't. They rely on the adults in their lives to provide parameters and guide them in appropriate ways to behave.

Rules and boundaries are designed to keep children safe. Children are more likely to respect limitations when they understand the rationale behind them. They need to learn this from their caregivers.

Having rules and boundaries is effective if they are used in a consistent way. Children respond very well to being told that 'this is the way it is going to be' because they don't know any different. But when the rules are not consistently implemented, children

Children are more able to grasp rules and boundaries when they are explained in simply ways.

become confused and feel unsafe. If you are inconsistent about the importance of rules and fail to follow them through with the agreed consequences, then your toddler will learn to protest and test them more and more often. So what do you need to consider when setting rules and boundaries if you want your child to follow and respect them?

♡ **What rules are necessary?** The safety of your child is paramount, so many rules are made to ensure this – for example you must stay close to me/hold my hand when we are walking along a road. In addition, rules are necessary to help manage the smooth running of family life.

How parents can help Make reasonable rules for your child to keep, but don't impose more than are required, as your child may grow discouraged, and find it difficult to keep them all.

♡ **Are the rules simple?** Children need to be given straightforward rules so that they understand them – for example every time I use the toilet, I need to wash my hands.

How parents can help When making the rule, explain to your child the importance of and reason for it in a way that he will understand, such as: 'Washing your hands every time you use the toilet will keep your tummy feeling well.'

♡ **Are the rules fair?** Rules need to be reasonable and appropriate for your child's age, and applicable to other children when they visit your home.

How parents can help Be consistent in your approach, and take a needs-led approach to setting rules. This is important as different age groups may have different needs.

♡ **Do all the adults in my family apply the same rules?** You need to work out the rules set for your toddler with your partner. If there are any disagreements, then they need to be resolved before the rule is implemented. If your child is aware of disagreements, he might play one of you off against the other.

How parents can help Communicate to all individuals who care for your child what rules or boundaries you have set, otherwise this will lead to a breakdown in what you are trying to achieve with your child.

♡ **Does your child understand what will happen if the rules are broken?** Tell your toddler in an appropriate way he can understand why a rule is being made and what the consequences will be if it is broken. This will serve the purpose of helping your child set standards for judging his own behaviour and to reason things out for himself.

How parents can help Get your toddler involved in setting rules as much as possible, so it will help him understand why a rule has been set.

Children can also show their understanding of rules by the rules they set for themselves during play.

A fair balance

Family discipline has undergone a major shift over the past two or three generations. In the course of the twentieth century the pendulum swung from strictly enforced 'rules for the sake of rules' to the wildly permissive, do-whatever-you-like attitude. Both had major drawbacks, since irrational restrictions and a regime of punishment hindered a child's emotional maturity, while an absence of boundaries often led to insecurity and lack of self-discipline. Parents of young children today have to find not only a sensible middle way but also understand and cope with attitudes from earlier generations.

Dealing with disappointment

Having to deal with disappointment is part and parcel of life, and the sooner that children learn how to deal with it, the better prepared they will be to bounce back to their original level of happiness.

If your child never learns to handle disappointment, he may later react very badly when he doesn't get what he wants. It will affect his ability to get on with his peers and to cope with what life will inevitably throw at him from time to time.

Life goes on

Allow your child to express his disappointment, while at the same time reassuring him that life is still livable. Remember, a disappointment may be something big that affects all the family, such as a cancelled holiday, but might also be something apparently inconsequential on which your child has focused great expectations, perhaps without your even being aware of it.

If his behaviour threatens to become extreme, distraction is often remarkably effective with toddlers. For example, say: 'Let's go into the garden – we could feed the birds/water the flowers.' Offer something concrete, and avoid 'Let's go and see if ...' – because if that doesn't happen either it will seem like a double blow at a vulnerable time.

The reason why

Explaining a disappointment can help make sense of what may seem totally unfair. Your toddler may have asked to have a pet, but your home is not suitable. If his best friend has a cat, it might seem quite unreasonable that he can't have one too.

Children may react badly initially to disappointment, but eventually will learn to accept that at times the answer is no.

Role play is a good medium to help children learn how to deal with disappointment.

Explaining, in terms he can understand, gives a reason for the refusal and helps blunt disappointment – for example that you don't have a garden and cats need to go outside.

Looking on the bright side

Help your child see an alternative point of view. You might remark, for example, that it is a good thing we did not buy the toy because the legs would have broken with just one fall. Or not being able to go to the pantomime means he can have his friend to play instead.

Learning by example

Your child will generally learn by watching how you and the rest of your family manage disappointment. If he sees that sulking or shouting is the 'normal' reaction to having a wish thwarted, he will follow suit.

? QUESTIONS & ANSWERS

Q My 3-year-old responds very badly when she doesn't get what she is hoping for. How can I help her cope better?

A It is natural for anyone to react initially with sadness or anger when something expected or desired doesn't materialize. It is important for you to show understanding to her initial reaction, even if you think that she is being unreasonable. After allowing for this, you need to communicate an approach where disappointment is acknowledged and talked through, but not dwelt on. Cushion the impact by focusing on things that your child *has* achieved or obtained in the immediate past. Remember, she will be learning her own responses by what she sees around her, so you and other members of the family should look at how you handle and show disappointment.

Q We try to see that our 2-year-old gets what he wants because we don't like to see him disappointed. People tell us that we are spoiling him. Is this true?

A You may be able to shield your son from disappointment now by giving him what he wants, but things will inevitably be different when he starts mixing more with others. There could be problems if he cannot accept disappointment and has difficulty in giving and taking. To prepare your son for getting on well socially, you will have to work less hard at giving him what he wants all the time. If you begin to refuse his unreasonable requests, he may initially react badly, but you will find he grows to trust your judgement, and eventually accepts that there are times when the answer is 'no'.

KEY STRATEGIES

Maximizing positive behaviour

A flexible, adaptable approach to dealing with your child's behaviour can be more successful than maintaining a strict and rigid style of discipline, as long as you remain consistent to the basic boundaries you have set.

Some parents think that they have to follow through a particular approach to get their child to learn a principle. But different approaches work with different children at different ages. Parents need to see the world from their children's perspective if they want obedient children. Here are 10 points to bear in mind when trying this out.

O━ Understand their present need. Children have the potential to display extremes of challenging behaviour if their physical needs of hunger and tiredness are not met. This can be resolved very quickly if you recognize the cause of their behaviour. For example, when picking your child up from playgroup, you might like to take a healthy snack, such as a sandwich, as this is usually a vulnerable time when children experience peak hunger.

O━ Lower your expectations. Some behaviour may be defined as a problem when in fact it isn't. Is it reasonable, for example, to take a 3-year-old into a toyshop and not expect her to ask for toys? If she does, and starts to make a fuss when she doesn't get anything, then it will be quite understandable. Try to avoid exposing your child to situations that you know will make them vulnerable to behaving badly.

O━ Deal with the moment. Be prepared to adapt your approach to what will work for that moment. For example, sitting at the table during mealtimes in order to learn proper manners may be too vague for a toddler, but encourage them to do so by doing activities that will make eating at the table fun.

Children will respond better to specific instruction rather than being given general rules about their behaviour.

O— **Know their limitations.** During the preschool years, children are not able to hold on to complex ideas as well as older children, so they are unlikely, for example, to grasp the concept of tidying their toys away when they have finished playing. Keep it simple and give them straightforward instructions of what they can do to help.

O— **Enter their world.** Your toddler might be in the middle of a fantasy when you need him to stop and do something else. Before you insist that he listens to you, ask him what he is playing, and present the new event or activity as an extension of his play. This minimizes resistance but gets things done.

O— **Use distraction.** If, for example, your toddler decides that she wants to empty the bottom shelf of a supermarket when you are out shopping, quickly find something else to attract her attention. You'll find that she will lose interest in the shelf and become more interested in what you have to say or show her. A distraction like a spotting or counting game (How many other little girls can you see?) may last long enough for you to finish the shopping.

O— **Use praise and reward.** Young children respond very well to being praised and rewarded for behaving in appropriate ways. Telling him he has been good and why will encourage him to act the same way again. This is discussed in greater detail in *Positive communication* (pages 56–81).

O— **Manage stress.** It is important to support your child when he may be experiencing challenging situations, as this is bound to affect the way that he behaves (see box). Be alert so you can react in good time before the situation becomes distressing.

O— **Be firm.** There may be occasions when your child makes unreasonable requests and will behave

The use of reward charts is a good way of getting children to pay attention to being good.

Coping in times of stress

Bad behaviour, particularly if it is out of character, may be due to something that is worrying your child. Try to identify the cause of his stress. This will be easier if you habitually encourage him to express his feelings. The cause may, to you, seem quite trivial, but never laugh or dismiss it, as it obviously is a real concern to him. Show him you are there for him and suggest solutions while letting him know of your optimism and confidence in his abilities.

badly as a consequence of being turned down. On these occasions, you will have to be firm, to help reinforce what the boundaries are.

O— **Show appropriate behaviour.** Children pick up what they see around them, so if you want your child to behave in certain ways, then you will need to make sure that you are also upholding similar rules.

Positive communication

The importance of play

Play is an essential stage of children's development, and how well a child plays can predict how well she will do in school. Depriving children of play can have a serious effect on their ability to communicate.

For all young children, play is their main way of learning new things and practising new skills in a non-threatening environment. Through play they learn to talk to other children in a relaxed setting, and find out about building relationships, understanding others and co-operating. Play can also be a means by which children can compensate for the anxieties and frustrations they experience in everyday life. Watching your child play, and playing with her, can let you in on what is going on in her world.

A child who is given the opportunity to play will develop most of the skills needed to be successful.

Role play

Acting out the life they see around them often forms a big part of children's play. This might be 'real life' – playing house or doctors and nurses – or fantasy triggered by stories or their own fertile imagination. But even the play-acting princesses or jungle explorers will be coloured by life as they view it around them; they are letting you know what they have observed about how people around them behave.

Pretend play in the preschool years is generally an indicator of overall quality of adjustment and social competence. It will also act like a mirror, reflecting your own life back at you.

Creative play

Before the inhibitions of the classroom and self-consciousness get to work, children are wonderfully creative in their singing, dancing and artistic endeavours. Encouraging these will provide valuable outlets for their self-expression and the release of strong emotions. As with role-play, your child will use arts and crafts to represent her world. For example, when she draws a picture of the family, she is letting you see her point of view.

Sharing

It is through playing with others that they will begin to learn sharing and co-operating, and achieving success as part of a team. Playing games together sets the foundations of the principles of taking turns and give and take, and even interacting through songs and rhymes helps build the idea of enjoyment through doing things with others.

Self-expression unleashes the developing personality. Creative play provides the perfect opportunity for this.

Q Since we emigrated, my 3-year-old son has been pretending that he is sharing his bedroom with his friend who still lives in our previous country. Is this normal behaviour?

A Yes it is. Many children make up an imaginary friend, but your son has conjured up one who does exist but is absent. The two were probably very close and got on well, and it is likely that your son is missing him very much, so his way of coping with it is to create an existence of his friend that brings him comfort. In time, when he gets over this separation and develops new friendships, he will abandon the pretence of his friend's imaginary presence.

Q When I see my 4-year-old playing, he doesn't seem to be able to focus for very long on an activity, unlike his playmates, and often just wanders off. What can I do to help him focus?

A By the age of 4 years, your child should be showing signs of being interested in playing with others, being able to co-operate and take turns, and able to plan how he would like to use his time in play. If he hasn't achieved this, then it is likely that he has missed out on some of his play development. By intervening early, it increases the likelihood that this can be corrected. You will need to continue to provide him with as many play opportunities as possible, and respond to his invitations to play with him whenever he makes them.

How children acquire language

Babies communicate without words from a very early age, but soon come to understand, before they can speak themselves, that language is a vital tool through which to convey their needs and find out about life and the world around them.

Children start to acquire language by what they hear, so they need to be exposed to a rich variety of words and expressions. Research shows that children's language development is enhanced by:

- A high level of parent–infant communication.
- Elaborating on early attempts, so they repeatedly hear back what they are trying to say.
- Being read to and talking about and discussing the story you are reading together.

In contrast, what can hinder a child's language development includes:

- A low level of parent–infant communication.
- Over-correcting a child's speech or punishing a child who does not perform according to your expectations of him.
- Isolation from others.

Surrounded by language

Children learn to understand words by the age of 8 months, well before they can say them for themselves. Their capacity for storing away this information is enormous, so as well as being spoken to directly, hearing a wealth of language from all sources provides an invaluable base on which to build a wide vocabulary and facility with language.

A two-way communication

Children are happy when the adults around them understand what they are trying to convey, so they are eager to learn to speak. Of course, early attempts may not be easily intelligible, so you will need to fill the gaps by trying to understand what message your child is attempting to get across. Picking up on body language and remembering what approximate sounds have turned out to mean in the past will help you interpret what they mean. Repeating the right words will help them learn faster. So, for example, say 'You would like a drink' in response to their request for 'gink, gink'. As their utterances become distinct, keep reinforcing how words should be said, and this will help their language to become sharpened. Children are great mimics, so if they hear a word or expression often they will strive to repeat it. Their love of hearing the same story over and over again is part of improving their language ability.

A good time to help children acquire language is during play, when you can introduce them to new words.

What you can **do**

Babies are born with an innate potential to acquire language. They need to be shown emotional warmth to bring out this potential.

Toddlers gain conversational skills through frequent, happy interaction with their parents and through their observations of other people communicating.

Saying nursery rhymes and singing songs help toddlers manage the flow of their words and tune into sound patterns.

Toddlers who are enthusiastic about books are well set up to be keen to learn to read for themselves at the right time.

Take your child out to various social situations.

Don't worry if your toddler frequently talks to himself. This is a good sign that he is getting to grips with this new way of communicating. Some young children will prattle away happily to a listening adult, whether or not their words make sense, while others are more reserved and then surprise you by coming out with quite complex complete sentences.

What you can **say**

Talk to your baby right from birth, to set his language development in motion.

Spontaneous play encourages a natural flow of communication, and daily routines such as feeding and bathtime build communicative relationships with opportunities for chat.

Have sing-along times, as repetition enables children to recall a song or rhyme and soon to start the singing himself.

Read with your child, providing a snug time for both of you to talk about the storyline.

Your child will pick up language when exposed to a range of conversations even when not directed specifically at him.

Take their level of communication at face value and reply to them, if appropriate, by paraphrasing or repeating what they say in clear language.

The importance of body language

Gestures and facial expressions are all part of communicating – indeed, much of what we convey is done without words. Children are effective users of expressive body language before they have the ability to say what they want in words.

When your 9-month-old smiles at you from the floor, and lifts her arms up, you know she is pleased to see you and would like to be picked up. When she settles in your arms, you know that you have a contented baby. All of this is communicated without words, yet you understand your child perfectly.

According to specialists, children are born with an inherent universal body language and they learn further actions as they develop. Babies use their eyes and limbs, in fact their whole bodies, to communicate in actions that are part of a learned and inherited vocabulary. For example, they soon discover that pointing works and results in rewards. They are also keen judges of facial expressions.

Learning from 'parentese'

Babies learn language more easily when adults use infant-directed speech or 'parentese'. An intrinsic part of this is exaggerated and dramatized body language. Babies begin to use it in the babbling stage, between 6 and 15 months, before they can say words. By the time they are 3 years old, most children's body language resembles that of the adults who regularly communicate with them. Bilingual children acquire the different forms of body language linked to their two languages and are rarely confused between them.

Children rely on body language as their means to communicate with others before they master spoken language. They feel happy when they are understood.

Babies and toddlers rely a lot on non-verbal means to get a point across before their spoken language is well developed, quite naturally adopting gestures and signs to overcome their inability to verbalize their needs and feelings. In turn, adults have to tune in to their children's body language, to interpret what they are saying.

Developing body language

Effort and time given to developing and responding to your baby's gestures make him feel good and teach him about communicating. This can be done by:

• Exaggerating and dramatizing physical movement, accompanied by stressed intonation.

• Being aware that your body language can act as a model for your child and is an effective way of teaching as well as communicating.

• Using books: picture story books can help to confirm babies' understanding of universal gestures such as smiling to greet, clapping to say hooray or hugging to show love.

Supporting the spoken word

Body language accompanies most human speech. It helps clarify meaning, emphasize important points and convey emotion. It is particularly important for children to use gestures for several reasons.

Gestures increase opportunities for deeper communication and improve bonding and the feel-good factor.

Research suggests that gestures increase and consolidate brain connections, which contribute to earlier talking ability.

Expressing themselves through their body helps babies and toddlers to dissipate frustration and tension – they feel listened to when their gestures get some reaction from adults.

When parents respond to babies' gestures by enthusiastically mirroring them and praising, it stimulates and helps them to acquire further non-verbal expressions.

Gestures can be especially helpful to boys, who are generally later verbal communicators and who also may need to alleviate physical frustration and stress.

Encouraging babies to make gestures is an important step to developing their speech. Babies who are encouraged to gesture get satisfaction and stimulation from their parents' enthusiastic responses, as it helps them appreciate the depth, power and joy of communicating, which in turn contributes to developing the ability to talk.

Self-expression

Expressing himself is an unfolding of your child's personality, which can be expressed in all sorts of creative ways, such as arts and crafts, making music, play-acting, pretend play and the re-enactment of experiences.

Young children have a refreshing ability for artistic self-expression that does not need to be taught or reinforced. In fact, research shows that if children are constrained from expressing themselves, their development of independent thinking can be affected. Children who are allowed to develop their self-expression will also develop the core skills of adaptability and flexibility of thought, which are critical for them as they grow older.

Means of self-expression

Providing an environment that allows your child to express himself artistically without undue constraints will allow him to explore and discover new ways of being creative. This doesn't mean you need to spend a lot of money on props. In fact, cardboard boxes and old sheets they can paint will fire children's creativity much more effectively than, for example, an expensive puppet theatre or a ready-built castle.

Self-expression should not mean complete pandemonium, paint all over the carpet every week and complaints from the neighbours. The trick is to set basic parameters but then allow your child full rein to explore an art or craft or play-acting as he wishes, without feeling he is being directed or quashed.

Prepare for a messy painting and gluing session by designating a suitable area or room and add to the fun by dressing the children up in plastic bin bags or aprons, or even no clothes at all; luckily these days most children's art materials are water-soluble and wash out. Noisy sessions are much more bearable and acceptable out in the open, and the park or the beach offer more opportunities for, say, full-blown battle re-enactments or invading Martians.

Communicating emotions

Art and music are just two examples of self-expression that are used as therapy after trauma; they are particularly effective as an alternative means of communication when, for whatever reason, expressing feelings in words is not possible. So it is not hard to see how toddlers might instinctively use banging a drum or drawing a picture of a monster to help release pent-up fears or frustrations.

Toddlers don't yet have either the vocabulary or the maturity to rationalize and tame their emotions. Encouraging your child to show his feelings through self-expression can avoid tensions, upsets or even happy feelings such as excitement becoming uncontrollable. Without playing amateur psychiatrist, as a parent you can learn a lot by looking at your child's forms of self-expression, whether it's dancing with delight or showing jealousy for a baby brother by painting a family picture and then scribbling him out. (See also Talking about feelings, page 70.)

What you can **do**

Be alert to how your child finds pleasure in self-expression rather than trying to structure his ideas to fit in with your own preferences or talents.

Be willing to get involved, and let your child take the lead.

Make the resources available that your child may need. She will also need help to organize things in a way that will provide easy access.

Try not to disturb children when they are in the middle of their creation, but offer some refreshment if they have been playing for a long time so that they do not get hungry (which can make them fretful).

Show that you value and consider what they are doing to be important, and praise them for what they have done.

Be alert to occasions when your child appears to be very emotional and upset.

What you can **say**

Ask: 'What would you like to do?' They may not be able to answer straight off, but they can give you fragments of insight and between you a suitable activity will be found.

If asked, say: 'Of course I will. What would you like me to do?' It is alright to make suggestions and negotiate as you go along. This will show your child that you are working as a team.

Remind your child of where things have been put if required. For example, say: 'Look, we keep all of the dressing up clothes in this box.'

Make a quiet entrance and say 'Here you are' at an appropriate juncture.

Say (of a performance): 'I thought that was excellent. I really enjoyed it,' or (of a piece of art or craft): 'Well done. You've worked hard at making that drawing look really colourful.'

Do not dismiss her upset as insignificant, but provide the opportunity for her to talk about it. For example: 'Why do you think you didn't draw this well.'

Providing choices and feedback

Choice, if not overwhelming, helps children develop their own personality and, in time, evaluate things for themselves. Children also need to be given feedback about their behaviour so that they know when they are doing things right.

Providing choices

Making choices makes a contribution to your child's emerging individuality. When she is allowed to choose today's outfit, for example, she gains a sense of satisfaction and feels happy. Children who are presented with very little choice, who always have someone else making choices for them, will miss out on developing their likes and dislikes. They will either learn to rely on others to make them for them, or put up with a situation that causes them much frustration. This frustration may show up in other ways, such as difficult behaviour.

Providing choices should not mean limitless choice, which has been found to lead to three major problems or difficulties:

Information problems. A child cannot be expected to access all information about all the alternatives in order to make an informed choice.

Error problems. With more complex options, a child is more likely to make errors in judgement and lose confidence in making a choice.

Psychological problems. Excess options to choose from can cause children to become overwhelmed. Instead of providing greater happiness, increased choice is accompanied by decreased happiness. Parents need to strike the right balance – just enough to allow your child to make a decision without too much confusion or discomfort.

Providing feedback

Giving feedback to your child helps him know how he is doing. A child who receives a mostly positive feedback will feel encouraged, while a child who receives mostly negative feedback will grow discouraged and begin to wonder whether he can do anything right. Of course, feedback needs to be accurate – you should not be positive solely for the sake of making a child feel happy, if a positive response is not merited. Children are often the first to know when they have done wrong. However, correction can be given in such a way that cushions the extent of negative feedback.

The goal of correcting children's behaviour is to teach appropriate social skills – not to punish the misbehaviour.

What you can **do**

Corrective feedback should always be supportive of your child, and focused on the undesired behaviour.

Deliver feedback as soon after the inappropriate behaviour as possible. This will help your child associate the behaviour with the feedback.

Acknowledge and express respect for your child's feelings. Children need to know that their feelings are valid and to have their feelings acknowledged.

Feedback should be specific and clear. Young children think in a concrete manner and do not always draw conclusions like adults. Children need information to be given to them in very specific and clear terms.

Always end on a positive note.

Be consistent with your feedback on all occasions so that your child can rely on your words.

What you can **say**

Say: 'You mustn't pull Emma's hair', not 'You're a very naughty boy.'

Say straight away: 'It is not OK to take away Peter's toy without asking him.'

For example, after a conflict you can say: 'I know that you were angry with Sharon, but it is not alright to punch her.'

Instead of just saying 'Stop it', say, 'Please don't talk to me at the same time that I am talking to David. If you want my attention, tap my leg and I will answer as soon as I have finished.' Always end on a positive note.

For example: 'You were wrong to take the pen away from John, but thank you for helping me put the pens away when I asked.'

Give the same message if an incident is repeated. For example, say: 'It is the same as before: no dessert unless you eat your dinner first.'

Using language effectively

Children need to be confident communicators in order to lead happy, fulfilled and successful lives. A child's ability to communicate is the basis of social and emotional wellbeing.

In order to have their needs met, to indicate their likes and dislikes, to make requests, to socialize and to establish and maintain relationships, children need to learn to communicate effectively. While, as we have seen in the previous section, body language plays a vital part in human communication, talking is at the heart of communication. Children who lack verbal ability will struggle in all areas. So how can parents tell if their toddler is showing signs of developing communication problems and what should they do to help?

Frequent natural interactions between parent and child will help facilitate language development.

Reasons for early communication problems

Early communication problems can be due to physical reasons or environmental reasons. Physical reasons include the presence of either hearing problems or brain damage, which may have been caused either at birth or through the development of an infection.

One source of evidence that a child is suffering from physical reasons is if they are quite delayed in achieving most of their developmental milestones. Parents will need to seek specialist help under these particular circumstances.

A parent has more influence on remedying early communication problems if the reason for them is environmental, as they can occur if a child has not been exposed to the type of interactions required to help facilitate language development, as discussed in the previous section. It is important to note, however, that children become competent communicators at different rates, and a lack of mastery of language should not be confused with early communication difficulties.

What are early communication problems?

Signs that your child may show if she has emerging difficulties include: an absence of the use of early utterances and subsequent word and sentence formation; a lack of awareness of the feelings of others; an absence of pretend or fantasy play; and a general inability to focus on an activity, such as approaching her play in a chaotic manner and using toys inappropriately.

A child can also be perceived to have communication problems when it is actually the circumstances she finds herself in that are the problem. For example, she may be asked to participate in a group activity at playgroup, such as a short performance, but because she has little experience of the activity in question she does not participate as well as she could.

Children need to be exposed to optimum experiences in order to increase their chances of developing the speech and comprehension skills required to communicate effectively in whatever situation that they find themselves.

Q We tend to speak in our own language at home, but our 1-year-old son will need to speak English once he starts school. Will this put him at a disadvantage?

A Whatever language you would like your son to speak, it is important that he is exposed to it before the age of 2 years. This period is a critical time by which children acquire language, and after this age they will pick up language at a slower rate. If you speak in your own language at home, then it would seem important for you to find other ways for your son to be exposed to English, for example by attending English-speaking toddler groups.

Q Our 3-year-old is still unable to form a sentence, even though most of his friends can. What am I doing wrong?

A Children tend to develop at their own pace, though there are certain things that parents can do to help maximize their child's potential in developing language. The first thing is that he should not pick up that you see this as a problem, otherwise this could hinder his development even more. As part of your natural interactions with him, you'll need to capitalize on those times that can provide opportunities for him to hear language. Make the most of story time before bedtime, and allow him to listen to you communicate with others. Elaborate on what he does say, so that he can learn new words to add to his sentence next time.

POSITIVE PARENTING

Talking about feelings

Young children, like everyone else, can experience a range of feelings in a day: some will be positive feelings and some will be negative. Children who learn to express their feelings openly will be able to resolve their conflicts more successfully.

Between the ages of 3 and 4, children experience tremendous emotional growth, and they begin to understand and label feelings. For a preschooler, learning to identify feelings is the first step towards managing them. When a child can correctly label her own feelings, she is better able to express herself and her needs. When children let their parents know how they feel, they can be helped to understand themselves and to cope with unhappy feelings, which is much more useful than repressing them (see box, opposite). So what can be done to help support open and safe expression of feelings in children?

♡ **Accept all types of emotional expression**
Children need to feel safe about expressing the full range of how they feel about different situations, the good experiences as well as the not so good. If they sense at any time that their parents are not interested, or they are punished for expressing strong emotions such as anger, they will become reluctant to share their feelings on another occasion.
How parents can help Pay attention when your child wants to tell you something, rather than putting it off until another time. Acknowledge and sympathize with her when she is either angry or upset, while at the same time advising on more appropriate ways to respond and communicate.

For children to be happy, it is important they are made to feel they can express their full range of feelings.

Encouraging openness

This is important for two obvious reasons. In the short term a child who has been able to get her message across will have dispelled her frustration and have fewer tantrums. In the long term, a child can soon become discouraged if she is left to deal with upsets and traumas without the help of an adult. If these incidents remain unresolved, they can build up to the point when a child can become affected psychologically. This can manifest itself in conduct problems and other challenging behaviour, such as aggression or uncontrollable temper. In fact, the encouragement of open expression of real feelings in children is said to prevent the need for psychological help, such as counselling, later on in life.

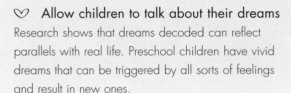 **Allow children to talk about their dreams** Research shows that dreams decoded can reflect parallels with real life. Preschool children have vivid dreams that can be triggered by all sorts of feelings and result in new ones.

How parents can help If your child experiences nightmares, as most do from time to time, you need to be understanding and offer comfort. This can take the form of a loving touch and soothing words until she falls asleep. Just being there and communicating your love in this way can alleviate the stress and anxiety of the fear she has experienced.

Ask them about how they feel Preschool children will encounter all sorts of new experiences and challenges, such as starting a new playgroup.

How parents can help Invite them to share their feelings with you about new situations. Once they learn to do this they will continue to use those discussions as a strategy to resolve their conflicts.

It is not the amount of challenging expressions that count. What is important is the making up.

Use story time Telling children stories provides a good opportunity to talk about feelings.

How parents can help While reading, talk about a favourite character and explore what that character may feel and why in different situations.

Use play Play acts as a good medium for children to practise their skills of communicating how they feel.

How parents can help Support children when they seek to play-act as different characters, and experience life as their pretend character.

Expressing opinions

A child's opinion is one of the things that gives them individuality and confidence, and distinguishes one child from another. A child who is lacking in opinion will go unnoticed.

Whenever you ask, 'What do you think?' you are creating an opportunity for children to show you how they make sense of the world based on the experiences they have had and what they have observed. You'll be amazed at just how much they have picked up for the small number of years that they have lived. They may explain what they know in simple ways, which will leave you in wonder, and

Group activities provide the perfect opportunity for children to learn how to express their opinions.

you may find yourself saying, 'Why didn't I think of that?' The more practice children get at expressing their opinions, the better and more confident communicators they will become.

Added confidence

Children who feel comfortable expressing their opinions will be at an advantage in getting along with their peers compared to children who cannot. If, as they grow up, children are not accustomed to forming and expressing their own opinions or having them acknowledged, they will look to others to provide them, and such children are more vulnerable to being led astray or being dominated by stronger personalities who find it easier to take the lead.

Encouraging opinions

For some children, expressing their opinion can be a daunting prospect, especially if they think that what they have to say is not important. But there are ways in which parents can encourage them, and the home provides a safe place to start:

Family mealtimes provide a good time to engage in lighthearted discussions that involve expressing opinions and exchanging ideas.

Focus on simple, everyday things with which they are familiar: 'Which flavour of ice-cream do you like best?' or 'What would you like to wear today?'

Set an example so that he can see others giving their opinions: 'Sam says he likes red best and I like blue a lot. What's your favourite colour?'

Make sure your child is clear about what he's being asked. As the playgroup question opposite illustrates, a routine question may hide all sorts of complexities or difficulties for a toddler. Children's ideas are not always feasible ('I want to go to the moon on holiday!'), but a child whose contributions are routinely dismissed or laughed at will become reluctant to express his views. 'Wouldn't that be amazing – maybe one day it will be possible for families to go to the moon' is a more encouraging response than a dismissive 'Oh yeah, now who's got a *proper* idea?'

? QUESTIONS & ANSWERS

Q How can I help my son develop the confidence to express his opinions as he gets older?

A Children naturally want to talk, and will develop their confidence as communicators if they are given encouragement. This can be done in a range of ways. Whenever he has something to tell you, give him your undivided attention, and ask simple questions to help him elaborate upon his story. This will make him feel that what he has to say is important. Also, help your son to develop a social life with like-minded peers, as this will provide plenty of opportunities for him to practise giving his opinion. Your son will look to you as his model, so create opportunities in your everyday conversations to tell him your thoughts about experiences you have had that he might find interesting.

Q Whenever I ask my 3-year-old about how she spent her day in playgroup, she never seems able to tell me. How can I encourage her to do this?

A Children will usually shut down if they are bombarded with questions. 'What did you learn today?' can be quite a complex question to decipher, because to children, they are not learning, they are just having fun. At this age, you will glean more about what your child has done in a day if you watch her while she plays. Children generally re-enact what they do in a day, and by observing her, you'll gain a lot of insight into how she played with her friends and some content of what the teacher will have said to the children. In addition, she will talk to you in her own time about scenarios that have made an impression on her.

Giving praise

Toddlers need to be praised quite a bit. During this phase of their lives they are still learning about what is acceptable and what is not, and praise reinforces your approval.

Young children offer plenty of opportunities to praise them: celebrating their achievements, acknowledging what they have done well, thanking them for being helpful and telling them how pleased they make you feel. Praise makes us feel good, and for young children it can:

- Help motivate them to act appropriately.
- Encourage them to learn.
- Set a standard for what they can achieve.

The right praise at the right time

When children approach the age of 4, they seek to please their parents, and when they know they have done so, they feel happy. A child who is praised for appropriate behaviour will become motivated to please his parents.

It is better to offer praise as soon as possible, so that it is linked to the behaviour you wish to encourage. Your praise should also be tailored to the event or accomplishment to emphasize its sincerity. There is some evidence to suggest that if praise is over-used, and is out of context, it can actually demotivate children.

Opposite are some examples of how to make praise specific and meaningful. As well as words, you can use devices such as sticker charts for good behaviour or special achievements. These might record acts such as responding the first time that they are asked to do something or being kind to a friend or sibling. Rewards are also very effective but need to be handled in the right way (see opposite). They need to be specific and appropriate for the situation.

A child who has her efforts acknowledged will continue to work hard at mastering her new skills.

What you can **do**

What you can **say**

Be specific rather than general. Your child needs to know precisely what she is being praised for.

Your child's behaviour will become strengthened when she knows exactly what she is being praised for. For example: 'You did well to stay in bed' rather than 'Well done'.

Repeating the same words decreases their effectiveness. Use phrases that are appropriate for the situation.

Avoid overusing phrases such as 'good girl', 'good work', and explain your pleasure by saying, for example: 'I like the way you helped me in the kitchen today.'

Gear words of praise to your child's level of understanding and interest.

Use short sentences with your 1-year-old, whose language is still maturing.

Be enthusiastic and sincere. Your child will be able to pick up the sincerity of your enthusiasm and encouragement.

Convey to your child that what she is doing has value. Say: 'I would like to use your picture to decorate the kitchen wall.'

Initiate praise and encouragement whenever possible, rather than waiting for your child to request it. Such praise carries more weight.

If you know your child is tidying her room, it is more effective to tell her 'You did well to put away your toys' before she asks you to come and see.

Help your child develop an appreciation of her own behaviour and actions.

Comments such as 'You did that all by yourself' help children recognize the value of achievement of their own behaviour.

Focus on improvement and effort rather than on outcome, so that your child can learn that it is their hard work behind the task that matters.

Say: 'You must have worked really hard to draw that big picture' rather than 'That's a beautiful picture.'

Rewarding good behaviour

When children are made to feel good about what they do, then they will seek to do it even more. Over time, this behaviour will become established to the point of becoming automatic.

Typical toddler behaviour

Parents commonly experience similar types of challenging behaviour in young children. Many talk about how their toddlers: desire their own way all the time; have little tolerance of hearing the word 'no'; have difficulty getting on with other children or sharing; have difficulty responding to simple instructions; throw tantrums; are naughty; won't cooperate and do the opposite of what they are asked.

At this stage of their development, children are still learning about the rules of behaviour. In many cases, parents deal with odd behaviour by taking punitive measures such as telling them off, and offering time out. Rewarding good behaviour can be just as effective as punishing bad behaviour to get children to behave in more appropriate ways.

Children do not naturally know how to behave appropriately – appropriate behaviour needs to be taught to them.

Just being with your child can be reward enough to keep him on the task.

How reward works

When children are rewarded for appropriate behaviour, they will learn to behave in desirable ways. The more a child's good behaviour is rewarded, the less they will be attracted to doing things that are not rewarded.

The advantage that rewarding good behaviour has over punishing bad behaviour is that it encourages children to want to behave in more appropriate ways. Focusing on the positive is more likely to acknowledge the needs of the child, and it makes children feel good rather than bad.

Where possible, offer a reward for good behaviour accomplished rather than as an incentive: 'You put your toys away nicely, so now we can go to the park' ideally sends out a more subtle, but stronger positive message than: 'If you put away your toys nicely, we can go to the park.' The former is a natural reinforcer of good behaviour, whereas the latter may lodge the idea of not behaving well unless there's the offer of a reward. See also Types of motivation, page 118.

Q My 3-year-old son is very naughty, and deliberately tries to make life difficult for me. I find it really hard to see any good behaviour in him. I've got into a cycle of shouting at him. How can I break this?

A No matter how naughty a child is, there is always something good about him, if one tries hard enough to notice. This can be difficult when you have to deal with what seems like constantly bad behaviour. So turn the equation around: because you are not currently enjoying interacting with your son, your negative view could be influencing the way you relate to him. You need to start liking him again, for him to feel liked by you.

You can start this process by beginning to notice little things to appreciate. For example, if he hangs his coat up when he comes in, you can praise him for doing this. If he comes to you for a cuddle, reciprocate and tell him that you love him. These small positive interactions will help to motivate him to want to please you.

Q I am concerned that just focusing on my 2-year-old daughter's positive behaviour will not help her to learn when she has done something wrong. Surely, she will need to be punished when this happens?

A Focusing on your daughter's good behaviour does not mean that her bad behaviour should be overlooked. Of course, when she is naughty she will need to be shown what is unacceptable. Focusing on your daughter's positive behaviour helps her to develop a motivation to seek to please you by behaving in more appropriate ways, so that she will learn to rely less and less on being naughty.

Nurturing enthusiam

Enthusiasm is the force behind motivation; it is what makes your child interested in learning new things. Enthusiastic children are curious about what is going on around them and this questing spark is something to be encouraged.

Enthusiastic children will actively bring to their parents' notice what it is that they want to do or find out about. Parents need to capture these opportunities by responding appropriately to their requests so that their enthusiasm will remain alive; otherwise, if they are constantly put off, this could dampen their interest. Children's enthusiasms can range widely, encompassing activities such as sport, dancing or performing, passions such as reading or drawing and themes such as dinosaurs or sports teams.

Here are some ways in which you can help support your child's curiosity and enthusiasm for learning new things.

♡ **Showing approval** Parents who demonstrate their approval of their child's enthusiasm will motivate her to continue with her exploration, and help sustain her interest.

How parents can help Encourage your child to pursue her interest by agreeing to participate, and make provision for this. Reinforce this by commenting on either how well you think she has done, or how much you enjoyed getting involved.

♡ **Parental aspiration** While expectation of what your child can achieve has to be tempered by realism, research shows that children's educational attainments are associated with their parents' aspirations for their lives.

How parents can help Showing interest in how your child spends her time, identifying what she may need to develop those skills that she shows enthusiasm for and making provision for this. Be positive in your attitude to build encouragement and optimism, rather than being negative, which will serve to deflate enthusiasm.

♡ **A stimulating environment** Children are naturally curious and interested in what is around them. They need an environment that will feed this. It needs to suit the level and pace of their development, with the joys and strengths that come from mastering challenges as well as companions who share their interests, curiosity, depth of understanding and sense of humour.

How parents can help Don't make assumptions about your child's abilities or interests. Observe how they play, and notice those times when your child loses interest in certain activities. This is the time to move them on to a more challenging activity, otherwise they will grow bored and lose enthusiasm.

♡ **Parental attentiveness** Children need the full attention of their parents, as this will strengthen their enthusiasm and gives them the message that you really want to know about what they are thinking and feeling.

How parents can help If your child wants to interact at a time when you cannot be fully attentive, let them know and schedule a time for conversation and/or play so that you can focus entirely on them. Your child will know if you only half listen to her and can feel frustrated and unheard.

Sharing in your children's enthusiasm will help them feel valued and give them the message that they are important.

Misdirected enthusiasm

If your child shows enthusiasm for something in which you already have a talent or interest, it can prove a great bond, but beware of taking the lead. Showing support and enthusiasm can, subtly, turn into demonstrating your own knowledge or ability, which may, without you realizing it, load expectations on to your child before she is ready. There is also a danger of making it seem less 'her' interest, and setting up a conflict between her wanting to please and wanting to assert her own individuality.

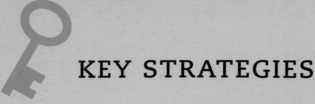

Recognizing clues to development

Children's behaviour patterns are constantly changing, because of the fast rate at which they are developing. You therefore need to be aware of when a change is taking place so that you can make adjustments to the way you relate to your child.

Remember, your child is communicating to you all the time about his needs and what works best for him. However, the message might not be obvious because of the way it's put across. Here are 10 strategies to help you recognize and act on the clues that your child is giving you at different stages.

Follow their lead. You may find that you are struggling in certain areas to meet your child's needs – for example with the way you would like to organize his time. Try following his lead, or listening to his suggestion. This may not be your way of seeing things at first, but you may be surprised to find where you end up; children are themselves often the key to what they can do.

Take their claims seriously. Your child might make a request to do something that you think is beyond his capabilities. But such a request generally means that they are ready to learn. For example, if he expresses a wish to play a particular game, don't hold back – you'll probably find that he has mastered the game in a few days, to the point of becoming unbeatable. If your child's requests are frequently declined, he could end up missing out on learning new skills.

Be alert to uncharacteristic behaviour. Preschool children communicate through their behaviour. If their behaviour is out of character, it generally means that some aspect of their need is not being met. Find out what this is, and deal with it straight away.

Create motivation. Whenever your child makes a reasonable request to do something, for example to be read a story, try to make time for this promptly, because he is developing an interest that will remain with him for life.

Cushion stress. A stressful environment will threaten the happiness of your child and can cause him to behave in inappropriate ways. While it may not be possible to stop stress from happening, there are ways to reduce its effect on your child.

Answer all those questions. Children ask a lot of questions because there is a lot that they want to know about in going through the process of making sense of the world. Don't get irritated by this. Remember that you will be making a contribution to your child's intellectual development every time you answer their questions.

Coping in times of stress

Bad behaviour, particularly if it is out of character, may be due to something that is worrying your child. Try to identify the cause of his stress. This will be easier if you habitually encourage him to express his feelings (see *Positive communication*, pages 56–81). The cause may seem trivial to you, but never dismiss it, as it obviously is a real concern to him. Show him that you are there for him and suggest solutions while letting him know of your optimism and confidence in his abilities.

Your child will let you know when she is ready to learn something new.

Take notice of unusual requests. Sometimes, your child will ask you to do something that you know he can do for himself, for example brushing his teeth or feeding himself. This does not mean that he is regressing, it's just a way of saying that he would like you to get involved on this particular occasion. He could be telling you that he is tired or he needs to feel nurtured. Be responsive, and you'll find that he'll get back to normal the next time.

Respect their suggestions. Your child might make a suggestion of something that he would like to happen, for example to invite a friend around to play. This highlights his level of sociability. The invitation might not work out, but at least he should know that you tried and that his request was listened to and not ignored. This will encourage more communication and suggestions.

Interpret crying. Babies have different ways of crying to mean different things. As you get to know your baby, you will learn what these are and be able to respond accordingly. Pay attention to non-verbal communication and body language.

Don't ignore persistence. There may be occasions when your child shows great persistence about something that you may have been ignoring for a while. When he keeps bringing it up again he is letting you know that what he has requested is important to him. By responding to his reasonable requests, you are letting your child know that he can rely on you to respect his wishes.

Getting along with others

Family and friends

Family and friends provide toddlers with their first social world, and it is through them that they derive a sense of security outside your arms and begin to learn to build attachments to people other than you.

Your baby's first attachment may be solely to one or two people who have been bonding with her since birth, but as she regularly encounters others who love and nurture her, and are sensitive to her needs, she will form other reassuring attachments.

Degrees of attachment

As highlighted in *Establishing a secure base* (pages 26–55), a secure attachment makes your toddler happy and relaxed. When she is with you and people she knows well, she will be happy to play. However,

the moment you leave, she will begin to cry and get upset, at least initially, but will not necessarily cry the whole time. This crying at parting is said to occur when a child has a secure attachment to her caregiver.

Young children who do not get soothed when their parents return and cry for prolonged periods are said to show ambivalent attachment. This stems from having experienced unpredictable swings between enormous affection and being rejected or being ignored. This makes children very anxious and needy as they feel the love bestowed on them is unreliable.

A third group of children, who appear on the surface unaffected by a parent's or carer's absence, and actively avoid contact on return, is said to show an avoidant attachment pattern. These reactions usually develop when children are exposed to a lot of stress within the home.

A lasting effect

Research suggests that the types of attachments babies and toddlers make affect their personality and view of the world as adults. Secure children grow into adults who find it easy to get on with others, are trusting and trustworthy and have high self-esteem. Children who form only ambivalent attachments are inclined to grow into anxious, preoccupied adults, while those whose experience has been of avoidant attachment patterns may become dismissive adults who keep their emotional distance and find it uncomfortable getting close to other people.

It is possible for children to become attached to several people as long as they are loved and nurtured and have their needs met by them.

? QUESTIONS & ANSWERS

Q My 1-year-old cries uncontrollably whenever I try to leave her with a friend. What can I do?

A Although your daughter's reaction must make you feel unable to do anything without her, be reassured: this is quite normal for her age. It is a sign that she is securely attached to you. It would be worrying if she did not show any sign that she was unhappy about the fact that you are not around.

The extent of your daughter's reaction, however, might be linked to how familiar your friend is – being left with someone she doesn't know well is likely to add to her distress. A period of visiting your friend together may help, so that your friend becomes a familiar face. Your friend can also help to settle her by, for example, playing with her with one of her favourite toys.

Q My 4-years-old still gets distressed when I drop him off at the nursery. Is this normal?

A Understanding the reason behind your son's distress is halfway to resolving it. First, think about whether he is adequately prepared to function at his optimum at the nursery. For example, did he have his full quota of sleep, and have a good breakfast? These things are important to give him a good start to his day. Secondly, do you have a sense of whether he has a lot to look forward to at nursery? Does he have special friends and are there particular things he enjoys doing there? If not, you may need to talk to the staff. Your son feels most secure with you and at home, and a nursery should be able to offer him something that can at least match what he gets from home.

Getting to know new people

With a secure relationship established with those closest to them, toddlers can widen their circle. Meeting new people can be exciting and enjoyable, but can be also a source of anxiety for a young child who is not socially confident.

Facing the world

Many children start to show interest in other children as early as 18 months, but all preschoolers are still at the very beginning of learning how to get on with others. Around this time your toddler will start to develop in ways that help him face the world with confidence: he now sees himself as separate from you and will be happy to be left with others if he understands the rationale behind it. Children learn to trust those people in whom you show trust, and are happiest in consistent and sustained relationships with other children.

New horizons

As your toddler begins to crave the company of other children, he will show excitement about the prospect of having visitors. At the age of 3 and 4 children start to understand social skills such as sharing and being kind, but can practise these skills only when they are feeling safe and happy.

Children will need to get to know new people all the time: whenever they start a new activity group, such as swimming lessons, or getting to know their parents' visitors or start at a playgroup or nursery. This can be a daunting prospect for your child, especially if he does not know what to expect. Whenever your child is faced with the challenge of meeting new people, it is important to think about how you can make the experience safe and enjoyable.

Children will usually learn to get on with those people whom they observe that you get on with.

What you can **do**

Prepare your child by taking him to those places were he will need to get to know new people.

Plan a reducing system. For example, stay the whole time for the first week, half a session the next, until all you need to do is take him and he will be happy to stay.

Demonstrate appropriate behaviour by showing an interest in interacting with other people.

Inform other adults about your child's likes and dislikes so that they will know how to relate to them and show sensitivity to his needs.

Do not undermine your child's sense of burgeoning independence if he tells you that he does not need you to stay.

Allow him to talk through his concerns so that between you a strategy can be developed to fall back on if required.

Help your child see the benefits of getting to know new people.

What you can **say**

Tell him what to expect: 'We are going to visit a new children's group to see if you will like it,' and the positive things: 'There will be lots of toys to play with and some nice snacks to eat.'

Tell him of your intentions so that he will not get any unprepared surprises: 'I'll stay with you today, and if you get on all right I'll only come for a little while next time.'

Praise your child for the times when he is able to get along with others.

Tell your child what you have said. For example: 'Sally knows that Rabbit is your favourite toy and that you prefer apple to orange.'

Say: 'That's fine, I'll be waiting here when it is time to pick you up.'

Say: 'So you haven't made any friends yet? This will take a while, but you've got your birthday coming up, so perhaps we can invite some children from your nursery.'

Talk about other occasions when she got to know new people and was happy to have done so: 'You got to know Bibi, when you started at the toddler group.'

Learning to empathize

Very young children are naturally egocentric, but as toddlers they begin to learn about the feelings of others. To understand someone else's feelings as if they were your own is an essential skill in getting on with others.

Empathy in children

Your baby starts off thinking that the whole world revolves around her and that her needs are the only ones that exist. Between about the ages of 3 to 4 toddlers begin to understand that other people have their own view of the world, and feelings separate from their own. The ability to show empathy will manifest itself the moment your child sees that someone else – you, for example – is upset and be affected by it, perhaps showing caring behaviour by stroking you and asking you whether you are alright.

The importance of empathy

Along with knowledge, self-determination and strategy utilization, empathy is coming to be regarded by more educators as a key attribute of a successful learner. In fact, as shown in *Understanding the happiness formula* (pages 8–25), showing empathy forms one of the elements of emotional intelligence.

To have empathy will also put your child at an advantage when making and keeping friendships. This strength will enhance your child's ability to adapt her behaviour to meet another child halfway, help her to be more patient and help her to be more under-standing and less demanding.

Tapping into your toddler's empathy can also be used as a useful tool to help her behave in desirable ways in your everyday interactions with her. Toddlers typically want to do the opposite to what they are asked to, but will quickly conform to your wishes, the moment they see that you may be upset by this.

Learning to empathize with other people's feelings can predict how well your child will get on with others in life.

What helps, what hinders

Some things that can help develop empathetic understanding in children include:

- Positive parenting practices.
- Reasoning with young children.
- Showing empathetic and caring behaviour yourself.
- Helping children identify when they have caused distress to others.

Things found to stunt the development of empathy may include:

- Using bribes or threats in an attempt to improve behaviour.
- Inconsistent reactions to children's emotional needs.
- Parental rejection or withdrawal in times of children's emotional needs.
- A home in which the father physically and verbally abuses the mother.

Children who play cooperatively find it easy to make friends and settle more quickly at school.

Q My 3-year-old son is very possessive with his toys whenever other children come to play with him. Should I stop inviting other children to our home?

A If you stop other children coming to the family home, then this will only curtail your child's development of learning to share with others. He needs to learn about ways that will help him to manage the situation. You could start by demonstrating appropriate behaviour to your son. This could involve you playing with him and his friend, so that he can see how you interact with other children. This will eventually lead him to approaching his play in a similar way. In the meantime, if your child continues to refuse to share, you need to give him explanations of how it will make his friends feel and suggestions for how to make amends. He also needs to be told about the effect of his behaviour on others and the importance of sharing and being kind.

Q I would like my daughter to become a caring person. How might I be able to help her develop her caring side?

A Children need first to develop an awareness of their own feelings before they can understand the feelings of others. You can help in this process by asking your child about her various experiences. This natural interchange will provide an opportunity for her to remember what it felt like.

Role play provides another opportunity for her to experience life from another person's point of view, so encourage any activities such as playing at nurses or looking after pets, where your child gets to be a caring character.

Caring and sharing

Learning to take turns and share are important social skills – children who can co-operate in play, negotiate effectively, compromise and win and lose graciously have a huge advantage when making friends.

Sharing is extremely hard for a little child. As far as your toddler's concerned, his own needs are more important than anyone else's. He thinks of everything as 'mine', and it takes quite a long time for him to learn that some things belong to other people, or that possessions can be shared.

Give and take in play

Most play involves taking turns and this is generally a much easier concept for children, since it implies you can have a go at something without compromising ownership. Children usually begin to acquire sharing and turn-taking skills between the ages of 2 and 3, generally mastering them by the time they are 5 years old.

Giving without any guarantee of receiving anything in return requires a supreme act of confidence and trust on your child's part. He wonders what is in it for him – in fact there is no immediate payback, although he will gradually realize that there is a positive value in friendship to be gained from being kind and co-operative.

Put yourself in your child's shoes

Your child may feel extremely attached to objects that you consider unimportant. Before you get annoyed, just think how you might feel if you were expected to share your car, jewellery or other prized possession.

When childred care for others, they learn that they are not the only one with needs.

What you can **do**

Research shows that even young babies demonstrate turn-taking by interacting with their parents and responding to positive attention.

Give lots of positive reinforcement by playing give-and-take games with your baby. Teach your baby and toddler by example.

Set limits for sharing. If a child finds it hard to understand 5 minutes, you can count out loud or set a timer.

Don't force him to share before he is ready, or take away a toy to give to another child, as this can lead to terrible tantrums.

Sharing involves trust – your child needs assurance that he will get his toy back and in the same condition when he shares with others.

Teach him to be able to play with his friends' toys and return them when he has finished.

Allow your child some control over his things and leave out only those toys he is happy for others to play with. He may be more willing to share if he doesn't think that everything is up for grabs.

What you can **say**

Talking back to your baby in between his babbles will familiarize him with the concept of turn-taking, laying the foundations for later turn-taking when he begins to talk and engage in conversation.

Emphasize turn-taking by saying things like: 'One for you and one for me', 'Roll the ball to me and I'll roll it back to you', 'Now it's Mani's turn, then Harry's'.

Introduce the idea of time and waiting, for example: 'As soon as I've finished the washing up I will help you with the puzzle.'

Mention the expectation to share and give lots of praise when he does: 'I was pleased that you let Tom share your sweets'. 'You played very nicely today. You are a really good friend because …'

Show your child you understand how he feels by saying: 'I know it's hard for you to share your toy, but Sam will give it back soon.'

Suggest strategies, such as 'If you want to play with Jay's toy, try asking him nicely for it'.

Accord special status to treasured possessions and give him choices. Ask him, 'Which toy are you going to let Joshua play with first?'

Harmony with siblings

Sibling relationships often gets talked about in the negative. It is commonly assumed that brothers and sisters will not get on, but this does not have to be the case. Understanding family dynamics can help avoid problems.

What lies beneath sibling rivalry is the perception of threat due to the differences that naturally exist between brothers and sisters. Family dynamics mean that children can be treated differently because of their age, gender, temperament and position in the family. It is not these factors in themselves, however, that cause the rivalry; it is to do with how they are managed. Here are ways in which parents can behave to increase the likelihood of siblings getting on well.

Families that pay more attention to the times when siblings get on will invariably promote more harmonious relationships between them.

♡ **Set up an expectation** Construct a reality that brothers and sisters will get on in your home, and seek to form a strong family identity of getting on with one another.

How parents can help Use positive language regularly with your children – for example, 'We know that you will be able to play nicely together.'

♡ **Develop a lifestyle of sibling harmony** Try actively to support those times when your children appear to be playing well together.

How parents can help Do not disturb your children when they are playing co-operatively, relish the

A good way to build caring friendships between an older sibling and a new baby is to let them get involved and help you.

moment, and do what you can to help build on it. For example, offer some refreshment to keep them going on this vein for as long as possible.

♡ Accentuate the positive

Before you begin to pronounce that your children do not get on, begin to notice those times when they do get on. You might be surprised that they get on more than you think. **How parents can help** Show your children when you are pleased with their behaviour towards each other and it is likely to make them want to get on well together more often.

♡ Don't make comparisons

Children who regularly hear how their sibling is better than they are in certain areas will soon grow discouraged, and this could set up conflict between them. Everyone has strengths, and it is the task of parents to identify the unique strengths of each child; don't expect them to be the same.

How parents can help Acknowledge what each child is good at, and communicate this to everyone without implying criticism of the others – for example: 'Rosy did well to help set the dinner table, while you made a good job of putting away all your paints.'

♡ Facilitate but don't interfere

It is important to acknowledge the expression of strong emotions between siblings, such as anger, as this will help them to work through their differences rather than to suppress them.

How parents can help Judge when it is safe to allow siblings to settle their own differences. Only when it becomes necessary, facilitate an open discussion between them to reach a satisfactory resolution of the conflict.

The new baby

If you are expecting another child, set up the expectation that your toddler will get on with the new baby rather than thinking the opposite. The non-verbal messages that you will give out as a result, for example by involving her at every stage, will cause her not to see her new brother or sister as a threat, but rather as an asset.

A new baby is often thought of as a potential source of difficulty for other children in the family. However, children are generally pleased when they have siblings, as these form their first friendships, and many only children will, even in adulthood, express a wish to have had a brother or sister. Young children quickly pick up on tension within the family, and are more likely to identify the idea of 'a rival' or 'not getting enough attention' if you yourself are preoccupied with these thoughts.

Learning to co-operate

Co-operation is the ability to work together with others, and to show willingness to be of assistance to someone else. It is another core skill that will enhance your child's ability to get on with others successfully and develop friendships.

Children show evidence of being able to understand the simple basics of co-operation from about the age of 8 months. You can see this when you ask your baby to let you have a toy he is holding and he gives it to you. Although children are born with the potential to co-operate, their preoccupation with their own needs can sometimes get in the way. The more exposure they have to situations where they need to use co-operation, the more they can practise it.

Practising co-operation

Communicating to a toddler in age-appropriate ways will increase the likelihood of him being co-operative. Instructions need to be kept simple and specific to ensure he understands what is being asked of him. 'Go and tidy your room' is too vague and complex. Instead, say, for example, 'Put all the balls in the basket.' Build fun into co-operating – for example, 'Let's count how many coloured balls we can pick up from the floor.' Reinforce with praise all attempts that your child makes to be co-operative, and let him see you being co-operative in a way he understands as well; he will model his behaviour on yours.

This also applies in groups. Participating in group activities with other children will present him with opportunities to see co-operation at work and to learn about co-operating with others. Research shows that co-operation can encourage trust, sensitivity, open communication and sociability.

Direct refusals

When children refuse to co-operate, it is important to understand why. It may be that they do not have the ability to do what is being asked of them. Or the request was not packaged in a way that appears attractive for them to do. Gentle facilitation will help you unravel what will help in these circumstances.

Children are more likely to cooperate if they can see how it will benefit them. This will be the case if what they are asked to do has an element of fun in it.

Q Our 2-year-old does exactly the opposite of what we ask. How can we help her become more co-operative?

A A 2-year-old will not have developed all the skills to react to formal verbal requests. Keep instructions simple and specific, and introduce other forms of communication, such as play. Suppose one challenge is to get her dressed in the morning. Try a paradoxical approach, such as 'Betty, watch *me* put *your* clothes on!' Before you know it, she will be running at you to claim her clothes back. She needs to feel that there is something in it for her, and clearly the element of competition in this example will act as the incentive. When she co-operates she will see that it feels nice and will aim to continue.

Q When my 3-year-old is involved in playing, it is the hardest thing to get him to move on to the next phase. How can I make these times less traumatic?

A Interrupting anyone engrossed in a task is unlikely to go down well. Children respond very well to being prepared. In addition, they are likely to be more co-operative if they think that what follows is an extension of what they are involved in. For example, if your son is pretending to be a teddy bear, he may not even respond to his own name. If you say something like, 'Teddy, we need to buy some food at the shops so that your other animal friends can come for tea,' this kind of seamless extension will put a big smile on your son's face, and you'll be surprised at how co-operative he will become.

Positive play

Play is the main occupation of a toddler, and a big part of their normal development. During the preschool years, your child will use play to communicate and much of what he learns will be done through play.

Stimulating the imagination

Playing is not about buying the latest high-tech toys; it is about creating the right environment to unlock your child's creative potential. For example, imagining a box as a boat and the sofa as an island is going to exercise his imagination far more satisfactorily than having everything handed to him on a plate ready thought out.

Learning through play

You will notice that your child probably likes to play-act everyday life he sees around him. Pretending like this is fun, but it also helps him make sense of what he observes. He may wish to use grown-up items to assist them in the creation of this make-believe, for example using your pots to make food, so accommodate him as far as it is safe to do so.

Having fun and being relaxed while playing makes children more amenable to learning, while anxiety will impede your children's learning. This can happen when they are expected to behave in ways beyond their developmental level, for example being forced to learn to read. When children are introduced to learning in a fun way, then learning becomes an activity that they look forward to rather than dread.

♡ **Understand their perspective** Parents need to see the world from their child's perspective, to appreciate the importance of play in these valuable times of development.
How parents can help Spend time playing with your child, and you will gain insights into the way he thinks and sees the world.

♡ **Develop a 'playful' lifestyle** Young children respond very well to interaction when it is packaged in a fun way, so work at finding the fun in your everyday activities in order to sustain their interest.
How parents can help You may not be able to play with your child on his terms all the time, but you could make games out of adult activities, such as baking cakes together, and competition games, such as how many pairs of socks you can make.

A feeling of freedom

Play provides children with a world of possibilities where there are no limits, which suits them just fine, as being subjected to limits is one of the areas where they can experience their greatest anguish. During play, for example, your child can be the parent and you the child, which can give him a feeling of authority that is never the case in reality.

Play is the main occupation of every toddler. It is during these times that they let you know what they have learnt about the world.

♡ **Be flexible** Parents need to adopt a flexible approach in order for children to gain maximum benefit from their playtime.
How parents can help There may be occasions when your child's play leads you both in a particular direction, and the two of you are getting so much out of it that you don't want to stop at the scheduled time. When you can, leave the routine behind, and go with the flow.

♡ **Make the time** Some parents feel that they do not spend as much time playing with their children as they would like. There is always something else to do.
How parents can help Just do it, and see what a positive difference it will make to your relationship with your child.

♡ **Allow them to take the lead** It is important that your child feels as though he is taking the lead while he is playing. Remember, play is about his learning and discovery, and not yours.
How parents can help When you are playing together, let your child tell you what to do, rather than you taking the lead.

Responding appropriately

To respond appropriately, a child needs to have understood and be able to execute what is being asked. Children are more likely to respond satisfactorily when you relate to them in ways that make sense to them.

Every parent strives towards getting their children to behave appropriately, but almost every parent is faced with challenging behaviour in their toddlers, particularly when they hit the 'terrible twos'. It is at this age that life seems to offer maximum frustration and difficulties, most often because of wrong assumptions and misunderstandings – on both sides.

A toddler's perspective

In order to maximize success in getting your toddler to behave appropriately, you need to understand her capabilities and stage of development, be sensitive to her needs and be able to see the world from her point of view.

A toddler may become truculent if she doesn't see the point of something, and verbal reasoning alone may not be appropriate. If your 1-year-old refuses to have her nappy changed, try telling her that you will put the nappy on her favourite doll instead. Soon she will want the nappy, and the attention, that her doll is getting. If your toddler frets at having her hair combed, make a fun competition of it, and ask her if she can count up to 10 before her hair is finished.

In general, young children are easily distracted, lose their concentration and forget what they are supposed to be doing. They need to be praised and congratulated for any effort they make in order to keep them motivated. As we have already seen,

During the preschool years play can be used as an effective tool to get children to respond appropriately.

What you can **do**

Spend time getting to know the way your child thinks: play together, and pay attention to how she understands the world, learning through the routine of your interaction together.

Participate in game playing to get your child to behave in ways that you would like. This will motivate her to becoming more amenable to your requests.

Provide opportunities for your child to exploit her potential. This will help promote her sense of feeling understood.

Use distraction. This can work very well if you want to distract a young toddler from behaving in inappropriate ways.

Tap into your child's empathy by pretending to be distressed by what she does.

What you can **say**

Respond to her enquiries, and engage with her in conversation as often as it feels natural to do.

'I wonder where Jo is?' you might say, if she hides under the blanket when it is time to get up, or 'Superman, please fly off and take this toy back to your bedroom.'

If, for example, she asks to open the front door with the key, let her try, provided it is safe. She may show that she can master an unexpected skill.

Ask her to get involved with what you are doing, for example: 'Help me fill the shopping basket.'

With a frown on your face, as if you are upset, say: 'Alice won't let me change her nappy.' Before you know it, because she cares for you, she will come in an obedient manner to have her nappy changed.

young children also relate very well to play, and this can be used to get them to behave in ways that you would like. Above are some further suggestions.

Frustrating times

Knowing that she has been asked to do something, but understanding imperfectly what, is frustrating for your toddler as well as for you, while not being allowed to try something she thinks she can do is likely to bring on sulks or a fit of temper. Of course, toddlers' wishes often outstrip their ability, but if their safety is not at risk they can often surprise you with the speed of their learning and their tenacity. This time in your child's life is a time of fast development, and you need to keep alert to adapting your responses to their behaviour and actions accordingly.

Coping with conflict

Children are not born desiring conflict. If parents assume that children are being intentionally aggressive, they will begin to expect their child to behave in undesirable ways, and the child will become labelled as difficult.

Growing pains

It is little wonder that early childhood can be a time of upsetting conflict. Toddlers have to cope with many different aspects to their development, which can make them behave in ways that could cause conflict, especially if you are unaware of the cause. For example, boys experience a testosterone surge around the age of 4, which can lead to boisterous behaviour. Also, young children's frequent growth spurts can put their routine out of sync, which can cause problems for both them and their parents.

Intellectual development outstrips even physical development in these early years, and toddlers are keen to test themselves. Psychologists call this self-efficacy. If children are always put off, it can discourage them from trying and they may become angry and upset and begin to challenge their parents.

Learning to cope

An ability to deal with potential conflict has its roots in early family interactions. You can help by:
• Being aware of your child's developing needs. An understanding of what is behind her behaviour will help you manage it more successfully.
• Offering help in a non-judgemental and constructive manner.
• Discussing causes and consequences of interpersonal conflicts in an age-appropriate manner.

Playing and learning with other children presents challenges and provides critical opportunities for learning to manage conflict.

Whenever children play with others there is potential for conflict. These occasions should not be avoided, but should be managed appropriately.

What you can **do**

Show understanding and help your child to understand for himself the triggers behind his confrontational behaviour.

Offer support and encouragement for replacing aggressive behaviour with more acceptable ways of behaving.

Help your child develop conflict-solving strategies.

Help trace how a conflict with a sibling or peer started so that they can explore other ways of getting the desired outcome.

Help your child to identify and verbalize his feelings and those of others.

Teach your child to ask for assistance whenever he is in difficulty.

What you can **say**

For example: 'You're a bit tired at the moment, let me take you for a nap, and then you can continue what you are doing later.'

You might say: 'It sounds like you have both had enough of this game. Shall we do some painting now?' Show understanding by offering an alternative: 'If you have had enough of this game, then let's go and watch television for a little while.'

Suggest a face-saving solution such as 'How about if you take it in turns to mix the cake?'

Say: 'How come you both needed to start shouting at one another?'

Start with an opening statement such as: 'Do you think that Jane would like to come and play with you again?'

Give him examples. Tell him that he might say, 'Tony won't share the game with me.'

Managing emotions

Emotional management is not about eliminating troubling emotions – it is about learning how to gain control over them. Managing emotions helps children be more successful in social relationships and in their communication with others.

During the preschool years, children rely heavily on expressing how they feel through their behaviour, and the outward expression of their emotions can appear more exaggerated than how they actually feel. For example, a 2-year-old who cannot have the expensive toy in the shop can scream as if she were being burnt at the stake.

Getting along with other children is another area that needs much emotional control as toddlers learn to share and co-operate. Young children will have quite a lot of emotion management to do, especially as life does not always go the way that they would like. Experiencing emotions such as frustration, tension and anger is therefore an inevitable consequence of learning how to behave appropriately with others.

Feeling better

Below the age of 3 years, children behave as if there is nothing that they can do about being upset, but as they get older they will become more amenable to finding a way to make them feel better. Exercise and music are known to soothe and lift the mood, and, as children are naturally social beings, interacting with others in a positive way is another route to a brighter mood. Additionally, as a child learns to deal with his emotions, he most likely will be capable of helping others to deal with their emotions.

The more children are exposed to activities that make them feel good, the more they will learn to manage their feelings.

What you can **do**

Research shows that exercise can make people feel good. Build various forms of exercise into your child's day.

Teach your child to give herself 'pep talks'.

Tap into the calming effect of music: allow your child to listen to music regularly. You can make it a habit to have music on in the background when your child is playing.

Organize time for your child to play with children with whom you know she gets on well, for example by inviting the child and her mother to a picnic.

Pleasant distractions can also serve to lift the mood. Create opportunities for your child to engage in focused activities, such as arts and crafts, that she likes to do.

Ensure you know how to manage your own emotions when around your child. Children pick up what they see around them.

What you can **say**

Make her aware of how the exercise benefited her, for example: 'You seemed grumpy before swimming, but now you're all smiles.'

Show her how she can do this, by saying something like: 'It's alright that you didn't get that doll. You've got lots more that you can play with.'

Have sing-along times with your child, as she will find this immensely enjoyable.

Tell her what you liked about this time together: 'We all really enjoyed playing chase in the park after the nice picnic today, didn't we?'

Participate with her and use the time for some child-led conversation.

Avoid talking to your child about your problems. At this age they are unlikely to understand what is going on.

Developing emotional resilience

The ability to maintain a positive outlook, bounce back from setbacks and recover quickly from negative emotions is something that helps every young child, and such resilience makes a lasting contribution to personal growth and development.

Research shows that positive emotions such as enjoyment, happiness, playfulness, contentment, satisfaction, warmth, friendship, love and affection all help enhance resilience and the ability to cope in the face of adversity. Feelings like this allow you to make a positive reappraisal, or infuse negative events with positive meaning. Being able to do these things in turn facilitates bouncing back fast after an unpleasant event. Moreover, the development of certain strengths helps build resilience and buffers against some types of psychological problems. These strengths include: optimism, courage, future-mindedness, faith, hope, honesty and perseverance.

On the other hand, negative emotions such as discontent, envy, loneliness, sorrow and dissatisfaction all decrease the ability to see the positive side of life or to leave bad things behind in the past.

A fine start

As highlighted in Bonding with your baby (see pages 28–9), when children develop secure attachments, this helps to set them in the direction of developing emotional resilience in later life. These reassuring attachments, coupled with paying attention to

It is inevitable that children will have set backs, but an emotionally resilient child will bounce back.

There will be times when children get upset. What matters is that they don't stay upset.

maintaining their happiness, is just what is needed in order to help children achieve emotional resilience.

One core area that makes children happy is to play. It has been found that the positive emotions associated with play can build physical abilities and self-mastery, increase enjoyment of times with friends and develop social skills. Even though the emotions themselves felt during these activities are temporary, the important physical, intellectual, social and psychological resources that they engender are enduring throughout life.

Furthermore, just as negative emotions can lead into a downward spiral into depression, positive emotions can trigger an upward developmental spiral towards improved emotional wellbeing.

? QUESTIONS & ANSWERS

Q My 4-year-old daughter has difficulty in adapting to change, and with making new friends. What can I do to help her cope when she goes to school?

A Is your daughter used to interacting with other children? If not, then maybe she experiences difficulty because she has not had a lot of practice. Regularly invite round children with whom you know that she gets on well, so that interacting with children is a familiar part of her life. Children feel comfortable with new situations and friendships if they feel safe and happy, so look back to previous situations that have involved change to see if you can see what might have made her feel insecure.

Starting school can be a daunting prospect for any child, so show her you understand this. Offer her reassurance of how much you will remain involved. Visiting the school a few times will help it become familiar. If you know of another child who will be starting school, invite her around once or twice beforehand. Knowing someone in the classroom can often take the edge off anxiety.

Q My 3-year-old seems to be a generally happy little boy, but how can I know for sure that he will remain happy as he grows up?

A Be reassured. If your son is happy then don't question it, just enjoy him, as it is more than likely that you are doing all of the right things. Of course, having to cope with life's complexities can't be avoided; it is an inevitable consequence of being human. But the fact that your son is happy now is a good sign, as happy people are more able to cope with whatever life throws at them.

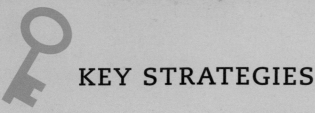

KEY STRATEGIES

Fostering positive experiences

Learning to pay more attention to the positive things that takes place in their life helps young children develop an ability to look forward to new challenges, rather than facing them with apprehension.

Already, as a toddler, your child is beginning to learn that life has its ups and downs. As the previous section has shown, the positive or negative attitude with which we face problems or difficulties will influence how they affect us and how well we overcome them. Laying up a store of positive experiences as a child is an excellent bolster towards coping with what life throws at us later.

Here are 10 keys ways in which you can help provide your child with these positive experiences and contribute to later happiness and resilience.

O— Prioritize close friendships. Your child is likely to get more out of the friendships that she can build on. Quality is better than quantity. Seek to organize occasions in your child's week when she can have time to play with her friends.

O— Provide new experiences. Children like to go out and enjoy age-appropriate activities. Make use of opportunities for events set up specifically for children to attend.

O— Savour the moment. When you notice your child getting on very well with someone or in a particular situation, seek to build on this experience. Sometimes a little memento can be the perfect reminder. A mother once described how she was having a lovely quiet time with her daughter, much enjoying each other's company. Then her daughter asked her to wait while she left the room. She came back with a drawing to give to her mother, as if to

When children are introduced to new experiences they become less daunted by new challenges.

say it represented a continuation of their time together, a reminder that would last longer than the moment.

O⊶ Act on your child's requests. There may be occasions when your child makes a request to go somewhere or do something, for example a visit to the library. Be prompt to act on her requests when this is feasible. This will not only make her feel happy, but will help her to develop an ability to choose her own activities rather than just going along with someone else's suggestions.

O⊶ Comment on successes. There may be a lot of failures that you can identify in your child's behaviour, but equally there are bound to be a lot of successes as well. You need to pay greater attention to the successes than the failures and communicate this to your child so that she can develop a positive sense of self.

O⊶ Sharpen talents. There are a lot of activities on offer these days aimed at helping children develop particular skills, such as learning ballet, playing an instrument or playing sport. Encourage your child in the ones for which she shows enthusiasm, as these opportunities can give a big boost to her confidence.

O⊶ Encourage helpfulness. Praise your child for the times she is able to show helpfulness towards others. She will gain an inner glow at having been able to help, which will add to the positive feelings she has about herself.

O⊶ Introduce the idea of positive reflection. It can be beneficial at times to help your child reflect on what is good about her life, as this can help develop a sense of gratitude. For example, 'You're lucky to have a baby brother that you can play with' or 'I can see that Tina is really pleased she's got you for a friend.'

Those special times that children share together will last for more than just the moment itself.

O⊶ Adapt to change. Children's behaviour patterns and needs are very changeable, so you will need to be aware when this is taking place and adapt your approach to respond accordingly. This will help your child feel at ease and cared for.

O⊶ Spend time with one another. Make time to get involved with your child, and their world. They will be happy to play games with you, and doing this creates opportunities for the two of you to laugh together and create many happy memories.

Getting along with others   107

Developing confidence

Overcoming fears and anxieties

It is not unusual for young children to develop fears that focus on a particular object or situation. Some of these are quite normal and reflect how well your child copes with certain situations; others have no rational basis but are no less real.

Rational causes of fear or anxiety in toddlers include strangers, separation from their parents, loud noises, new and unfamiliar situations, a change in routine and perception of harm being done to someone close to them. Being forced to do something prematurely can also cause deep-seated anxiety.

Irrational fears – spiders, lightning, a monster under the bed, crowds, the dark, going to parties – often develop if your child perceives the object or situation as a threat. This can arise if he has either experienced a real trauma because of the object of fear or has built up negative associations. Being startled by a clown in make-up might build up into a fear of going where there might be clowns. More commonly, irrational fears are picked up from other people – if you are very nervous in thunderstorms, for example, your child will learn that thunder and lightning are to be feared. Helping children overcome their anxieties and fears needs to be done according to their level of development.

A child's uncertainty regarding new situations is a very normal reaction to coping with the unknown.

A child who is gradually exposed to what he fears or is anxious about will overcome it in the long run.

Dealing with irrational fears and anxieties

In general, the way to deal with an irrational fear of a particular situation or object is gradually to expose your child to the situation (see the spider example, right). It is good to become aware of situations of which she could potentially develop a fear, and nip it in the bud as soon as possible, otherwise prolonged avoidance will cause the fear to become established.

Dealing with rational fears and anxieties

It is important to recognize that these are normal reactions for a young child, so they should be treated with much understanding and not be punished for it. These anxieties, many of which are to do with facing the unfamiliar, generally resolve themselves over time, as your child gets used to a situation or becomes familiar with a new setting or person.

? QUESTIONS & ANSWERS

Q My 4-year-old is petrified of spiders. How can I help him to get over it?

A Gradual exposure is the key. Your son has learned to perceive spiders as a threat, so he needs to unlearn this and begin to see them as harmless. You might begin by obtaining some pleasant stories about spiders being friendly and read them to him. The next time you see a live spider, do not make a big deal about its presence but convey to him that they are harmless. When he shows fear, offer reassurance and understanding and tell him that it won't hurt him. At a later stage of exposure you might take him to a zoo where he can learn about different spiders and their habits and usefulness. Don't force him to progress too quickly through the stages. Keep at his pace, wait for him to let you know when he is ready, and spiders will in time no longer be a problem for him.

Q My 3-year-old is normally a good talker, but becomes shy and hides away whenever we meet new people and they ask him questions. How can I help him to become more confident about talking to others?

A It is quite normal for young children to be unsure of strangers; they need a period of getting to know a person before they warm to them and begin to feel safe enough to talk freely. In addition, talking to others is a two-way process, and his reaction may have something to do with the way adults talk to him. Do they talk about what he finds interesting, such as his favourite cartoon, or do they talk to him from an adult's perspective? He is more likely to talk to them if they show some knowledge of his world.

Boosting self-esteem

The value that children place on themselves, and how much they feel they are valued by others, is determined by the messages they receive about themselves, first of all from their parents.

The feedback that children receive about themselves in their early years can determine the way in which they see themselves in later life. Developing a good self-concept is a motivating force towards higher aspirations and achievements. But what are the right types of messages to give your child that will help her develop positive self-esteem?

♡ **You are loved and wanted** There is some evidence to suggest that children can pick up on their parents' feelings towards them from the time they are in the womb. Children brought up in homes where they feel they are not wanted will become vulnerable to low self-esteem and as a consequence could develop psychological problems in later life.
How parents can help Tell your child often how special she is to you, and show her that what she wants and does is important. It is vital that your child feels she is a priority.

♡ **Your enthusiasms are valued and respected** A child who is exposed to an environment rich in play, and introduced to a wide range of activities, such as music, group activities and

When children are allowed to express themselves in ways that come naturally, they feel valued for who they are.

creative activities, is more likely to discover what she is good at and this will allow parents to note those activities about which she enthuses.

How parents can help Follow your child's lead in what she shows enthusiasm for, and make provision to help her build on these skills.

Some parents get discouraged if their toddler shows little interest or aptitude in doing a particular activity they are 'supposed' to enjoy, such as arts and crafts. You will bring out the best in your child if you allow her to experience a wide range of activities and avoid working too hard to get your child interested in doing something she clearly has no interest in.

♡ **You have done well** Children need to be told that they are doing well, rather than being told about what they are not doing well. Some children may not be angels, but parents can pay more attention to the positive things that they do rather than focusing on the negative things.

How parents can help Tell her what you liked about her behaviour whenever you can – for example, 'I liked the way you were able to sit with your baby sister and play nicely with her.'

♡ **You have natural strengths** Research suggests that knowing and following your strengths helps develop confidence, brings a sense of fulfilment, generates optimism, helps achieve goals, provides a sense of direction and encourages insight and perspective. Playing to your child's strengths can point her in the direction of achieving these.

How parents can help Recognize those things that your child does well, and communicate them to her and the rest of the family as a valued trait. For example, your child's inquisitiveness might make it a joy for you to feed her hunger for knowledge, or she might have a particularly empathetic nature, which you should praise.

Being introduced to a wide range of activities provides lots of scope for children to discover their strengths.

The negative in perspective

It's always much easier to point out the bad rather than the good. But remember that toddlers still have a huge amount to learn. Children do not deliberately 'wind up' their parents – they always do things for a reason, so you need to understand the reason before you judge their negative behaviour as a problem. What that reason is may not immediately be clear, which is why it is so important to work hard at learning the signs and behaviour traits that your toddler uses to express needs and wants and moods.

Managing frustration

Frustration can present itself in many guises, but it arises from difficulties that cannot be overcome. This occurs very often in the life of toddlers, who are learning fast, but whose eagerness to do things can exceed their ability.

Nearly every day your toddler will be faced with new challenges. Some will undoubtedly lead to frustration – at not being allowed to do what she wants, at not being able to achieve a goal, at simply not understanding how something works or why something is. Often, she will take out her frustration on the object, on you or whoever is nearest, or just wail at the unfairness of it all.

Challenges and problems are part and parcel of life, and children can begin to learn to manage them from quite early on.

Dealing with frustration

Many frustrations have an obvious cause – throwing a doll across the room because its clothes won't go on or kicking the stair gate because it's a barrier to going upstairs. Offer help where you can, and try to provide stepping stones towards achieving new skills, as the answer to the jigsaw question opposite illustrates. Meeting efforts halfway can help overcome the frustration without removing the challenge. Dressing the doll, for example, might involve you putting one doll's arm into the coat and then she, copying you, puts the other.

Young children also experience other, less concrete frustrations that they may not be able to express easily. These may include not getting on with

The sooner children are taught how to manage their frustration the better prepared they will become to cope with what life throws at them.

Children are less frustrated when they are provided with activities that satisfy their interests.

Q Now that my little boy can walk, he opens every cupboard that he can reach. He becomes easily frustrated when I try to stop him. How can I distract him from doing this?

A Children at this age are naturally curious and have a need to explore whatever is around them. If you try to distract him doing one thing, then he will find something else that rouses his curiosity. During this stage, the best thing to do is to make adaptations to accommodate him, within reason. If he likes looking into cupboards, then remove all the dangerous or fragile items and leave items that are safe for him to take out and play with, for example plastic cups.

Q My toddler likes to have a go at puzzles, but gets frustrated when they either take time to do or she does not know how to go about doing a puzzle. How can I help her to be patient?

A Your toddler needs puzzles that are appropriate for her age and right for her level of ability. To begin with, give her puzzles that are very quick to complete, so that she will feel rewarded and have a sense of satisfaction. She will let you know when she starts getting bored with this type of puzzle and then you can introduce a slightly more challenging one.

other children, being made to participate in an activity or not understanding exactly what is being asked of them.

In these cases you need to work with your child to resolve the problem, rather than avoiding it. She may need some time to talk it through as she sees it, to diffuse her emotional response. Then a plan can be developed between the two of you that will help towards resolving the situation.

Providing a role model

Children learn by example. It is important to show them that you approach life's challenges as problems to be solved rather than threats to get angry at. Children's frustrated behaviour can be frustrating for you, too, but they need to see you coping, not returning like for like.

Developing assertiveness

Assertiveness is the ability to be confident and direct when dealing with others. Assertive behaviour reflects a child's developing competence and independence and represents an important form of developmental progress.

You may have heard the expression that 'children should be seen and not heard', but in fact they should be both seen and heard. It is important that children develop the ability to express their point of view early on, as their needs can often get overlooked simply because they are small. If children are taught that it is wrong to be open about what they think and feel, they may develop either passive or aggressive tendencies to compensate.

Passive, aggressive or assertive?

Children who evolve a passive stance by tolerating a situation they dislike or resent can internalize feelings of anger and resentment. They may become withdrawn or uncommunicative.

Children who compensate for their lack of assertiveness by becoming aggressive get their own way at the expense of others. This may show up as deliberate disobedient behaviour. If they feel people don't understand or listen to them, they can become aggressive towards adults, including their parents, or towards other children.

Assertive children feel safe to communicate to those around them in a direct way. This can prevent

Playing with other children provides the perfect opportunity for a child to learn how to stand up for their rights.

internal stress and the development of other mental health and physical problems. How can parents help their children to develop assertiveness?

♡ **Show appropriate behaviour** Children tend to copy the behaviour of those around them, so if you want assertive children you need to be assertive yourself.
How parents can help Develop an ethos within your home that encourages open, safe and controlled expression of your thoughts and feelings.

♡ **Provide the opportunity** Parents need to see the world from their children's perspective to be able to make sense of why they may behave in the ways that they do.
How parents can help When your child makes you aware of how she feels about something – for example 'I didn't like it when you told me off about leaving my shoes in the hallway'– grant her the opportunity to tell you about it as she sees it so that you can between you reach a satisfactory resolution.

♡ **Praise assertive behaviour** Whenever children show evidence of behaving in an assertive way, praise them for it, and this will lead to a strengthening of this behaviour.
How parents can help Praise your child for those times when you notice that he is able to behave in an assertive manner.

♡ **Encourage them to speak up for themselves** There may be occasions when your child informs you about an incident that he would like resolved – a confrontation with another child in playgroup, for example.
How parents can help Discuss the incident with him, and between you reach a decision on how the matter will be dealt with. You might decide you can both go and have a chat with his teacher tomorrow.

Parents can help children develop their assertiveness by listening to what they have to say.

Children's rights

You will find it easier to see the need to develop assertive behaviour in children if you can acknowledge that they have rights too. These rights include:

- The right to be loved and nurtured.
- The right to be respected.
- The right to play.
- The right to feel safe.
- The right to be happy.
- The right to be listened to, and taken seriously.
- The right to quality time with parents
- The right to express their feelings.
- The right to be themselves.
- The right to have friends.

You may be able to think of many others.

How success breeds success

Children are more likely to be successful when they are happy. In general, happy people tend to make use of the opportunities that present themselves and have the motivation to make things happen.

Motivated people persevere until they strike success. This builds their confidence, so they begin to believe in themselves and develop the ability to rise to every challenge. Not only do they begin to expect success, but they can pick themselves up relatively quickly and find other ways of succeeding if one method fails. How can this outlook be developed in children?

Types of motivation

Children can either be externally motivated or internally motivated. External (also called extrinsic) motivation is driven by outside forces, typically either in order to obtain a reward (such as a treat for tidying up) or to avoid punishment. Internal, or intrinsic, motivation occurs when a child does something for the sake of it, simply out of enjoyment and interest – for example doing a puzzle for the satisfaction of completing it.

Intrinsic motivation reflects the inborn human tendency to seek out novelty and challenges, to explore the world and to exercise capabilities. The more this type of motivation is developed, the less your child will need to be forced to do things. Supporting autonomy is important for the development of intrinsic motivation. Children who choose a particular action are more likely to appreciate the reason for it than if they feel compelled to do it.

Developing self-motivation in your child will set him on the path to being successful and happier, as the more life is guided by intrinsic motivation, the more fulfilling it becomes.

Children will be more successful in school if they learn to find enjoyment in what they do.

What you can **do**

What you can **say**

Allow your child to make reasonable choices and encourage his independent thinking by pursuing reasonable ideas.

Let her to take the lead, for example by saying: 'What would you like to do this morning?'

Avoid rewarding, forcing or cajoling your child to do desired activities. This may lead to a lack of responsibility.

To provide a motivation for an activity, suggest why it is fun, or provide a meaningful rationale, and empathize with your child. For example: 'I know that it will take time to clean up, but just think about how much fun we can have in all this space.'

Don't leave achievements unacknowledged.

Give plenty of praise afterwards.

Give plenty of encouragement if success is elusive; it's hard to be motivated if you're despondent.

Acknowledge their feelings, but remind them of something associated that they have achieved, for example: 'Sam may not have played with you today, but at least you played a game with Kieran.'

Engage your child in meaningful activities that serve a positive purpose or the achievement of which will be satisfying or rewarding.

Seek their help, for example: 'You can help to make the sandwiches for lunch.'

Respond promptly whenever your child shows an interest in doing an activity, if it seems reasonable to do so.

Find out what her needs are and work with her to achieve them. For example, say: 'I don't have any card, but maybe we can make some with this paper.'

Gaining independence

Preschool children work at gaining a level of independence and come to view themselves as individuals in their own right, while still being dependent on their parents. Successful progress in achieving this is essential for their happiness and later development.

Developing independence in certain areas is the primary task of children in the first four or five years of their life. During this time, for example, they learn to feed themselves, use the toilet and dress themselves. They also become competent walkers, acquire language and are more likely to take the lead in managing their free time.

Timing and taking time

Children naturally show signs of their emerging independence, but need support in doing things for themselves. This can sometimes be a challenge for you. For example, your 2-year-old may insist that she knows how to put her clothes on, but if left to her own devices will put on a number of items back to front or the wrong way round. But trying and getting it wrong is all part of the learning process, and practice makes perfect. Dressing and re-dressing may take longer, and you may need to hide your frustration and build more time into the schedule, but praising her efforts and allowing her, eventually, to feel triumphant rather than thwarted will be a step towards a more independent, self-reliant toddler.

So how can parents support their children's independence at the same time as taking their developmental level into consideration?

Allowing your child to have a go will allow him the chance to master a skill sooner rather than later.

What you can **do**

Recognize signs that your child is eager to move on a stage. She may start telling you 'I can do it.'

Make prompt provision for your child's emerging independence. An early example would be to allow your baby the opportunity to crawl in a safe place.

Allow your child to help you with 'adult' tasks, such as preparing a meal.

Provide her with time and space to have a go at a new everyday skill. Follow her lead, as this will tell you that she is ready to grasp new ideas.

Without threatening safety, don't always play it safe. This will help you discover the extent of your child's capability. For example, leave him without a nappy for a period to allow him to use the potty.

Expose your child to an environment rich in language and experience; he will subconsciously absorb information that will help him establish independence later.

What you can **say**

Praise her and offer her a balance of freedom and help: 'Good girl. You put your hand in there and I will put your other hand in here.'

Engage with her by asking her to fetch an item on the floor.

Interpret, say, 'I want to cook' laterally, by allowing him a level of involvement, such as cutting some soft vegetables with a blunt knife.

'OK, you have a try' if she expresses interest in doing up your shoelaces, and encourage her attempts.

Prepare him in advance, by saying: 'After swimming, I'll leave the potty in the sitting room so that you can sit on it whenever you want to use it.'

Speak to your baby using proper words rather than 'baby talk'. As his language develops, the extent of his vocabulary will coincide with what he has been exposed to.

KEY STRATEGIES

Unlocking potential

Children will develop to their full potential when they are provided with rich, stimulating experiences where they can use their creativity and be allowed to exercise some freedom of choice.

Children need the right environment and opportunities to bring out innate potential. For example, if a child is born with the potential to be an actor, he needs to be allowed the opportunity to do drama in order to develop these skills. During the toddler years, the potential in children unfolds itself at a rapid pace, so to be in a position to help unlock hidden possibilities

Children are on the road to unlocking their potential when they spend time doing what they enjoy.

you need to be able to recognize the clues and act on them. Opposite are 10 key strategies to help you recognize the clues and unlock your child's potential.

O— **Accommodate your child's natural curiosity.** Children are active explorers of their world, and this thirst for knowledge needs to be fed if they are to develop to their optimum. Try to accommodate your child's reasonable requests as much as you can. Children ask questions because they want to know the answers, not to make 'polite conversation', so answer all her questions even if it means that you have to look up the answers.

O— **Follow your child's lead.** There may be occasions when your child makes a suggestion that may not fit in with your way of seeing things, but if you follow it through, you may be surprised where you end up: a key that could unlock the solution to a challenge.

O— **Stand back and observe.** Sometimes parents try too hard to get their child to do things in a very particular way. If this has been the case, stand back for a change and watch how she does it: you may be surprised at her capability.

O— **Say 'yes', and not 'no'.** Whenever your child invites you to play with her, she is telling you that she is enthusiastic and has a readiness to learn something new. Capitalize on this, as every time you say yes, you are helping her towards acquiring a new skill.

O— **Create plenty of opportunities.** The more activities that your child tries, the more widely her repertoire of skills will develop. She will also discover her strengths early on, which is a good predictor of becoming successful.

O— **Provide variety.** Draw on a variety of appropriate books, puzzles and games that can be used to spend time with your child. They can help promote language development, the use of the imagination and logical thinking.

A child who has his questions answered promptly will be more ahead in his intellectual development than a child who doesn't.

O— **Encourage expression.** Participate in your child's invitations to play with words – for example you can play word games during car journeys and shopping trips.

O— **Manage family problems.** Problems within the home can inhibit a child from developing to her full potential. These need to be managed in such a way that they have minimal impact on your child.

O— **Provide a model.** Parents who fulfil their own potential act as good models to their children.

O— **Include your child.** Encourage your child to play a part in family decisions. Listen to his suggestions and apply them where possible – for example, he might like to include some items on the shopping list. This will help him realize that his point of view is important.

Index

Acknowledgements

Executive editor: Jane McIntosh
Editor: Camilla Davis
Executive Art Editor: Penny Stock
Designer: Geoff Borin
Picture Research: Taura Riley
Photographer: Russell Sadur
Production Manager: Martin Croshaw

Publisher's acknowledgements
The publisher would like to thank Holly and Charlie Coleman, Jake and Imogen Franklin, Theo Goff, Willoughby Hardwick, Zita and Unity Kingston, Illana and Ariel Long, Dominic and Cameron Maddock, Elspeth McIntyre, Samuel Ralph, Scarlette Russell, Harvey and Abigail Sangster, Kitty Shan, Patrick Spice, Oliver and Luke Spooner, Connie and Ellie Thorburn, Ashley To, Reuben and Evie-May Walsh and Daniel Wong for being such wonderful models.

Picture credits
Special photography: © Octopus Publishing Group Ltd/Russell Sadur
Other photography: Alamy/Real World People 23; /BananaStock 39